Moonlight in the Dark Night

Moonlight
in the Dark Night

By Taoist Master
NI, HUA-CHING

The Shrine of the Eternal Breath of Tao
College of Tao and Traditional Chinese Healing
LOS ANGELES

Acknowledgement: Thanks and appreciation to Janet DeCourtney, Frank Gibson and the students in the Atlanta Center for assistance in typing, editing, proofreading and typesetting this book.

The Shrine of the Eternal Breath of Tao, Malibu, California 90265
College of Tao and Traditional Chinese Healing, 117 Stonehaven Way
Los Angeles, California 90049

Library of Congress Cataloging-in-Publication Data

Ni, Hua Ching.
   Become the cloudless sky / by Ni, Hua-Ching.
      p.   cm.
   ISBN 0-937064-44-0 : $12.95
   1. Spiritual life (Taoism) 2. Spiritual formation. 3. Emotions.
I. Title.
BL1923.N535   1991   91-60708
299'.514448--dc20   CIP

This book is dedicated
to those who wish to enjoy balanced love
and a mind with clear emotions.

To female readers,

According to Taoist teaching, male and female are equally important in the natural sphere. This is seen in the diagram of Tai Chi. Thus, discrimination is not practiced in our tradition. All my work is dedicated to both genders of human people.

Wherever possible, constructions using masculine pronouns to represent both sexes are avoided; where they occur, we ask your tolerance and spiritual understanding. We hope that you will take the essence of my teaching and overlook the superficiality of language. Gender discrimination is inherent in English; ancient Chinese pronouns do not have differences of gender. I wish for all of your achievement above the level of language or gender.

Thank you, H. C. Ni

Contents

Prelude

"Tao is the destination of all religions, while it leaves behind all religions just like the clothing of different seasons and different places. Tao is the goal of serious science, but it leaves behind all sciences as a partial and temporal description of the Integral Truth.

"The teaching of Tao includes all religious subjects, yet it is not on the same level as religions. Its breadth and depth go far beyond the limits of religion. The teaching of Tao serves people's lives like religions do, yet it transcends all religions and contains the essence of all religions.

"The teaching of Tao is not like any of the sciences. It is above the level of any single subject of science.

"The teaching of Tao is the master teaching of all. However, it does not mean the teaching relies on a master. It means the teaching of Tao is like a master key which can unlock all doors leading to the Integral Truth. It teaches or shows the truth directly. It does not stay on the emotional surface of life or remain at the level of thought or belief. Neither does it stay on the intellectual level of life, maintaining skepticism and searching endlessly. The teaching of Tao presents the core of the subtle truth and helps you to reach it yourself."

Preface

The focus of this book is to help the readers to pass through and go beyond their emotional experience to attain spiritual development. Emotion has two sides: dark and bright, unpleasant and pleasant, unhealthy and healthy. Taoists have emotion, but only on the good side. If a situation pulls them to the dark side, they will not let it press their life down for very long. Maybe they will experience that emotion for a few minutes or a short while, but then they return to normalcy, back to being calm, centered and content once again.

There is no secret to basic spiritual attainment. One key is understanding that worldly life is a set of conflicts, if you do not choose to be pulled down by life and emotions, you need to keep pushing yourself up. Another key is to live your own life. Living your own life means that you do not live a life that somebody or something has organized for you, whether it be a sage or a stiff religious teaching. It means continuing to learn from the lessons of your life to gain wisdom so that you make good decisions by yourself. Living your life is not a kind of presumptuous attitude. Living life can best be done with an attitude of refinement. You achieve this attitude by personal spiritual cultivation.

Living your life as an emotional victim and associating all that happens to you with old emotions is a bad habit or weak spot in your life. Old emotions continue unless you are determined to live your own life. If you do not have the spirit of independence and self-determination within you, your emotions will always respond to other people's actions. Do not be affected by the junky thoughts you gather from your life experience or any external situation.

Many students wish that I would teach how to clear up emotions. On most occasions, I cheerfully and joyfully teach people. People are joyful when they come to listen to me, and I have many things to teach them. I do not discuss emotion to stir up people's emotion. This book is my response to some people's wish.

This book is dedicated to those who are in the stage of almost being ready to overcome an emotional problem. In these pages, you can find help and practical suggestions to assist your everyday life. Even on a dark night, you will still be able to see the bright moon, like the image I have when I work on my emotion.

> *The moon waxes and wanes.*
> *Tides ebb and flow.*
> *Emotion moves up and down.*
> *Only achieved ones enjoy*
> *The smooth flow of nature.*

Your spiritual friend,

Ni, Hua-Ching
January 30, 1991

Chapter 1

How to Heal a Broken Heart

In the place where I was born, winter is just ending at this time of the year. It is the twelfth lunar month in the Chinese calendar, which is equal to sometime in February in the western calendar. The Chinese calendar was dated according to coordinating the lunar cycle with the solar cycle. They are two different cycles, skillfully combined to become the ancient Chinese calendar. It is too soon for farmers to begin their busy agriculture work, and it rains a lot. The roads are slippery, so during this time of year all travelers need to take extra precaution. When I was growing up, some travelers rode horses, but the main means of transportation was to travel on foot. People walked wherever they needed to go around the whole country. People traveling on business and so forth tried to hurry home before the rainy time started. If they did not make it back in time, they would stay in a hotel. Thus, since married people or people with lovers could not see each other as soon as they wished because of the delay of the rain, they missed each other very much. Thus, the poetic people named this time of year "broken heart season." Things that are touched by poets tend to be a little sentimental. It is a very productive time for poets; both the rainy weather and the missing lover are inspiration for them. Ordinary people use this time to sweep the tombs of their ancestors. These are just a few of the interesting customs followed on the other side of the world.

Today I would like to talk about techniques that can be used to heal a broken heart. However, before we start, I would like to tell you that if any of you here today have a broken heart, this class can give you some guidelines for what to do. In general, it takes more than one day to heal a broken heart. Recovering from a broken heart is a kind of spiritual achievement. Once you are a totally achieved person - and by this I mean a person who can independently stand on your own two feet - there is no such a thing as a broken heart or even a bruised heart.

Generally speaking, people feel loneliness during their journey of life. The pressure of loneliness pushes them to look for a partner or mate to make the life journey more enjoyable for themselves and the other person too. This leads people to enter relationships. Sometimes a suitable relationship is the result, but sometimes people try to mate with someone who is an incorrect choice for them and trouble ensues within the relationship. However, the most frequent cause of relationship trouble is lack of proper balance.

If you are a strong, self-sufficient person, and if your relationship has trouble, your mind is already balanced so you will be able to make it through the storm better. Some storms clear up happily, but others end in disappointment.

Actually, disappointment in love is almost always a matter of a person losing balance. If a person's mind lacks balance in the first place, the person suffers and the person's mind suffers. This occurs not only in a broken heart from a relationship, but also in many other circumstances of life. It happens when a person's mind is not balanced.

A person whose mind is not balanced reaches out to others with the wish to take something or hold something. Such a person expects that this something or someone can support his or her balance. In other words, that person is not going into a relationship with the intention of taking care of himself and pulling his own weight.

If an unbalanced person is leaning on something, and that something goes away, the unbalanced person will fall. It is that kind of reliance or expectation towards someone else that causes a broken heart.

The best way to overcome a broken heart is never to get one. That requires a person to be able to gain and maintain balance. It means that every day and every moment, you are already working to keep the balance of your mind and heart. You do this first. You do it continually. If once you do not have this kind of balance within yourself, no medicine or technique can really help you. All you have to do is restore your mental balance which you have when you know that you are doing all right in life. It is when you know you can take care of yourself. You know that things may not always go smoothly, but you manage to make it through. You feel strong within yourself and can do whatever you need to do.

I would also like to point out that having a broken heart is not really 100% harmful. What is harmful is the imbalance that exists before the relationship even begins. It could be caused by your suffering from loneliness. You may have already built up an idea in your heart or mind that you need somebody to be your company. Once you establish a close friendship with someone, if you continue to stay close, the person becomes more and more significant. You must not have irrational expectations of the contribution that any one person can make to your life, however. If you do, you will probably be doomed to disappointment.

In most types of relationships, especially business, people calculate the profit or favor they are going to receive. This often happens in personal relationships too. However, relationship is not only getting, it is also giving. It is not wise to expect the profit. The other person may also expect the same.

The spiritual virtue of relationship is to fulfill one's own obligation but not have expectations of the other person. In reality, when people always look to see if the other side is meeting its requirements, and do not look at what should be fulfilled on their own side, disharmony occurs. People suffer for this all the time.

If you have a son or daughter, a husband or wife, can you always expect them to meet every want and need in your life? No. Such an unreasonable demand creates an imbalanced condition for a potential separation and broken heart. It is the cold reality that people live for themselves. If you have this understanding, you need to break away from too much demanding. If you are not ready for a relationship, first you have to work on not having the feeling of loneliness. You can do that by developing your emotional strength and independence.

If you want somebody meaningful in your life, that does not mean that you depend upon somebody to make your life meaningful. It means that your life is already meaningful to you; then maybe someone can share with you. If you feel your life is empty or lonely, it presents a condition that you lack the strength of emotional independence. It is a shame if you allow your emotion to develop into disappointment. This is the real trouble.

If you are disappointed in love, if somebody gives you up, or goes away from you, first you recover from the change in situation. It is not always a good idea to find a substitute person very quickly as a replacement.   If you are disappointed in yourself, then you have a good opportunity to see your shortcomings and work to improve yourself before you enter another relationship. This can probably save you from another broken heart.

It is important to be honest with oneself. Many people cannot admit their shortcomings to themselves, not realizing that when they know the truth, they can begin to free themselves from it. Staying blurry minded or blurry eyed is not helpful. Emotion makes a person blurry, not clear minded and with clear vision.

Let us talk more about loneliness. All people come to the world, but only a few are born as twins or triplets. Thus, aloneness is a condition of life. Aloneness is a state of being which is quite all right and for some people is quite enjoyable. Loneliness, however, is a pressure to most people. If you do not work on yourself, you always feel pressured by loneliness and you think that there are no people who understand you. Although individual life can be experienced as an isolated island, however, in the big sphere of life, it is vast like the ocean. I mean, it is actually vast like a continent in the big sphere of life, and you can reach out for a good connection. The only way you can truly establish a connection or relationship with another person is to change your idea and stop imagining yourself as an unreachable island. You can be a continent! Your life can hold as many lives as you choose, depending on how much you can expand yourself.

Practical spiritual achievement is not expanding yourself. The practical spiritual achievement is dissolving yourself. If you always put yourself first by thinking, "I am suffering, mistreated, have bad fortune," those thoughts are self-pity, not loneliness. If you feel you are friendless and so forth, it means you need some companions not a friend. A friend means more than just companionship. Surely, a companion can be a friend. A companion is someone who you spend time with. A friend is someone who also helps or supports you.

However, negative emotion has no end. It is you who pushes yourself to feel bad and be disappointed in yourself. You can change yourself to say, "I have come to the world. The world is an appropriate place for my spiritual growth. Before I came to the world, I was a bit of subtle energy, unshaped and unformed, but merged with the natural universal interplay of yin and yang."

Your mother and father, no matter who they are and no matter what their nationality, gave you the shape or form of your life. With this shape and form, you are incomplete psychologically, but spiritually complete. You need clear vision to understand yourself. How can you be psychologically incomplete and spiritually complete? You know, before you form yourself to have the opportunity of joining the interplay of yin and yang, you are shaped as a bit of energy. At that stage, there is no gender distinction of man or woman. Only during the formed life are you a man or a woman. Even though you are now man or woman, internally you are still complete. If sometimes you feel that some part of you is man, and some part of you is woman, it is because you do not have internal harmony. You do not recognize that even your formed life is still a transition.

For example, some people you like and some people you do not like. The fact that there are some people that you like means that your personal, internal energies are in a state of imbalance. It indicates internal disharmony to need a certain kind of person or type of friend. If it seems that the person can assist you to accomplish or complete your shortness or imbalance, this is the case. It is a kind of energy attraction. For example, a married couple consisting of a short woman and a tall man may be an energy situation in which each person accomplishes or completes the other's imperfection or imbalance. Internally, it may be associated with psychology. In a case where you need some external assistance or external help, a condition is built as a first requirement in looking for partner. After you have fulfilled your wish and you are assisted, then you see the shortcoming of the other person later. This new knowledge of yours causes trouble; you must look for a new adjustment.

Fundamentally, each individual needs to look for his own spiritual achievement, and not escape from recognizing his own shortcomings. If you achieve spiritually, it will help your mind. You will enjoy your life more. Otherwise, you may not like your life, because you feel you are always missing something. You are always looking for something. You always need something to help you, to support you as your crutch.

It is important for all of you to understand the feeling of loneliness, self-disappointment or self-pity. All those things you can feel are from your life environment; they are not descriptions of your true nature. Comparisons between yourself and your neighbors or friends, or with things that you see in the marketplace or on television make you feel that way. If you are spiritually achieved and one day you feel a little lonely, you say to yourself, this, too, will pass.

After people are around fourteen years old, they long for a friend of a different sex. Before, when they were little, boys and girls played together without any special interest in a particular gender. Afterwards, people find it hard to stay peaceful, because their sexual desire never feels fully fulfilled. They still wish that some day, that part can feel really fulfilled. By feeling this way, they are always looking for that other part, even when they come to be old. However, if your life is normal, then your demand for another sexual partner is much less when you are older. This kind of fulfillment is still incomplete unless you work on all the other aspects of your life and look for balance among them.

Maybe you are a very sensitive woman or man, and you are nervous about presenting yourself in front of someone of a different sex. In a meeting like this, you do not need to be sensitive about your gender, because you are learning something above the differences of gender. The person who is in this chair teaching right now could be a woman like you instead of a man. If you do not hold to a sharp sense of being a woman, your openness will enable you to enjoy a broader range of companions to reduce the problem of a broken heart.

A broken heart is a condition of psychological blockage that you accelerate or develop from your ordinary environment because you do not work on yourself, or have enough spiritual growth to know that that direction is not correct. You need to maintain your spiritual harmony and spiritual integrity without being pulled apart by the polarity of physical life.

A broken heart is a condition of stubbornness. Because you are stubborn, you do not give up the thoughts that you were hurt or abandoned by your lover. When I was young, my father told me a story. He knew someday I would make use of this to help someone. There was a young man who fell in love with the daughter of a rich family. At that time, the social structure was so tight that the poor boy was destined to be disappointed in love. The marriage could not take place because of his poverty. So he gave up writing poetry to pursue material wealth. He became rich and possessed many properties, especially much beautiful land. Then, he wished to marry the woman, but unfortunately she had already married somebody else, and she had died. The man suffered a broken heart from this. Before he became rich, he was refused, but now that he had worked hard to become rich, his lover was no longer alive.

He relieved his pain by walking in one of his own forests. Every day he walked there because of his broken heart. The forest became famous because of him; it was known as "the forest of the broken heart." Trees are natural; they have a power to cure a problem, so the more he walked, the less he felt his broken heart. He was cured by the trees, and no longer suffered a broken heart. However, the name "forest of the broken heart" stayed on. He changed the forest into a park, so that many people could go walking there. Many people with broken hearts spent hours walking among the trees. Actually, after some time, anyone who walked in that forest was said to have a broken heart, whether they did or not!

A long time afterwards, a young man suffered a broken
heart, similar to the one in the above story. He decided to
hang himself there in the forest of the broken heart. He
looked around so that he could pick out the right tree.
Finally he found a beautiful one, and said, "This is the one."
Then he took off his belt and tried to put it on the tree, but
the tree was too inaccessible. There was no place on that
tree where he could put the belt that would make it tight
enough to do the job. That make him so mad and unhappy
that he cursed the unhelpful tree.

A gardener working in the forest saw the young man
cursing and asked him, "What are you so mad about?" The
young man replied, "I have traveled a long way over here
just to hang myself on this particular tree, but this tree does
not help me." The old gardener kept walking, and calmly
said, "You have already decided to hang yourself. What are
you so mad about? If you would like to give yourself up, you
don't need to feel upset."

Do you understand? A person who has already decided
to take his own life should be calm. But this man chose the
tree; because the tree could not help him with the job, he
got upset. It is not necessary to hang oneself on a particular tree; he could have simply, calmly, picked another tree.
But generally people decide that their own death must be in
a particular way. If you have already decided to take your
life, why take so much trouble for anything, even to hang
yourself? If your spirit is really ready to face death, it is not
necessary to take too much trouble. Anything is okay. This
metaphor means that you do not need to die for a particular
person or a particular reason.

The gardener said to the young man, "You know, a
person like you who has enough courage to face death must
certainly have enough courage to take the pain of a broken
heart, which is much less." The young man finally gave up
his madness, anger and upset because the tree did not help,
and went home.

A place particularly known for this sort of thing has
many stories associated with broken hearts. Once a young
man came through the forest of the broken heart with the
same intent of ending his life. He also came looking for a

tree on which to hang himself. On that day, however, there was a little wind. He could see the trees shaking their heads, making noise and singing songs. When the man found a tree good enough for hanging, he heard a voice. The tree talked to him and said, "Don't hang on me, don't hang on me. Grow your own root."

My friends, do you understand? This means that you cannot try to hang your life on somebody else. If somebody wishes to give you up, you can accept that in a better way than by having great sorrow and emotion. "Okay, you give me up. I have my own root. I will do all right by myself." All of us need to grow our own root, and not hang on anybody. If you hang on somebody, and somebody suddenly gives you up, you fall.

Afterwards, some people peeled some bark off the tree and wrote, "don't hang on me." So people who wish to hang themselves on that tree find that there is no tree to do the job. They need to go home to grow their own tree. There is no tree anywhere that attracts you to hang yourself. It is your own madness.

You know, all human lives are like trees. We do not look like trees, but human lives are all similar to trees. We need to grow, and we need to develop our own root. This is not something that happens only in your mind. Many superficial or external things really cannot help you, especially when it comes to the deep sphere of pain in the heart. If you feel pain or trouble for something external, it means you really have not worked on yourself. You have not grown your own root.

To talk about growing one's own root is my subject. This is our work. Taoist teaching always reminds us that we need to work on our spiritual cultivation, to develop ourselves spiritually. That is the direction in which we grow our own root. Once we grow our own root, we do not need to hang on somebody else. Nor do we need to look for a tree to hang on. When you have your own root, you can grow your own tree. Success or failure, beauty or ugliness, shame or glory, regardless of what you feel, you keep growing your good tree. You extend your root farther and farther. You keep growing and ignore the momentary experiences of your life.

Do not hold in your heart the pain you call disappointment in love. Spiritually, it really means nothing. Psychologically, you can have a positive attitude that you can use this kind of situation to reflect the matter of life and human relationships. Then you can grow. With your growth, you develop spiritual understanding, the power that uplifts your life and keeps you moving in the right direction.

People who do not have spiritual understanding might mistreat people or become unfair or aggressive. Those people do not grow well spiritually. Spiritual people who grow well are very just, righteous, earnest and virtuous. Spiritual growth is not any different from strengthening your life. It is really worth working on it every day.

In this sphere of life, under the condition or law of polarity, we always feel good sometimes and feel bad sometimes. With a strong root, even in a severe, cold winter, you can survive. Every day you go out into society and experience different things. You like all good things to happen to you, but sometimes things happen that are not as you expect and you feel hurt. Why keep the feeling of being hurt?

So every night you go home and you check out your root. I tell you that your root is not hurt. What is your root? Your root is your life. You are still a healthy individual. There is lots of potential for new opportunities to happen in your life. Even if it is your last chance, and nobody loves you any more, you can still be happy. That is because nature guides you to experience your own seasonal changes. It means your life has cycles; it is not good all the time or bad all the time. Living is just like driving your car down a road. At some intersections, you experience traffic jams and cannot move freely. However, have patience; with a little time, the road itself will clear up for you. Then you can reach the destination you choose.

The most important thing in your life is not external gain or loss. As I described before, external gain or loss is momentary. Now you feel you need a gain, but you still will have other opportunities if you keep your root whole and deep and intact. You can still grow. People who are committed to personal growth use the times when they are in relationship to learn more about themselves as other people reflect back to them. They also use the time when they are not in relationships to explore different aspects of themselves. All situations are useful.

Sometimes I feel I am in too much of a hurry to teach you. I have worked here for ten years. Almost every day at the side of my busy complete Taoist medicinal practice schedule, I teach and write, and sometimes hold meetings. It is not that I think of myself as clever, but I try to offer my service to those who need it as part of my medicinal practice. I think it is time for me to recommend some practical methods for you to do. It is hard for people now to do practice, because all of you are intellectually developed. We ignore the spiritual side of life. We ignore even the natural truth and the effective methods that can help us reach the truth. Instead of integrating what we learn into our lives, we just sit and listen over and over again. Perhaps we think that the talking is more important than doing or being. That is not true. It is fine to sit here and think about things, but your true being is deeper than thought. It is your life. Your real being is more important than any mental or emotional projections you might make. Thought is just a picture passing through your head.

It is important for you to learn some of the things I recommend and teach in different classes of the College of Tao. For example, if you have a troubled mind, doing Eight Treasures or T'ai Chi movement will unite your body and mind.[1] They can relax you and help you become clear.

Most people's hearts and minds are not joined. That is the trouble of modern people. They do one thing, but they are thinking about something else. These special spiritual practices help people connect their minds and bodies. For example, when you drive your car, if you listen to the radio and sing, you have separated your mind from your being.

---

[1] *(The video tapes of these exercises are now available, see ordering information in the back of this book. - editor.)*

It is just like being cut into many pieces. But when you do the practice of T'ai Chi movement, Eight Treasures or other similar Taoist practice, you always unite your spiritual level with the mental level. The emotional level and physical level are organized in one place without self-robbery or self-theft.

I would like to explain the two Taoist terms self-robbery and self-theft. They mean that you steal something from yourself. Ordinary people always do things like causing themselves to have a broken heart. Some time after your spiritual achievement, you know that the broken heart is a kind of self-robbery or self-theft. You are the one who steals and harms your own heart; it is not somebody else.

You abuse yourself by continuing to think about the pain after the pain is already passed. The thing may have been finished for a long time already, but a person will still be holding onto that pain. That is to continually practice self-robbery or self-theft; you are stealing the good energy of your life and turning it into self-pity by feeling and thinking about pain. The part that enables you to think and feel is what we call your life energy. If you face a particular situation in life that you do not know how to handle, before you make another choice you need to refresh your mind to overcome feeling pain or feeling bad, which constantly press you down. There is a part of yourself that is capable of feeling and thinking things. That part is close to the center of life, and is more important than the pain put upon you. You can choose that part instead of choosing pain.

Your life energy is just like the paint brush in the hand of the painter. One can paint a beautiful picture or an ugly picture, or pictures of many kinds of things. It is all accomplished by using the one same brush. Your capability of feeling and thinking is like the paint; it is colorful, but the dynamic stroke of the brush cannot be seen. In other words, the paint can be seen, but not the dynamic, creative energy which moved the brush. The thoughts and feelings are close to the essence, but it is still not the essence of your life. Value the essence. Do not steal or rob it and turn it into pain. It is the life energy that enables you to live. That bit of energy can bring many positive things for the enjoyment of your life through your work. But if you misuse your energy negatively and feel pain and think pain, it is like squandering your material wealth for unimportant or unhealthy things.

So the Taoist terms, self-robbery or self-theft, refer to energy. Life itself is energy; it is a bit of chi. What you get from it depends on how you use it. Self-management or self-government could be common sense or ordinary understanding. A Taoist eventually needs to accomplish or fulfill his spiritual integrity. You are complete, you are balanced, you are harmonious.

In your life, if you discover yourself feeling pain or unhappiness, it means some part of you is not right. You have lost your balance. Immediately, you need to restore your balance. Whatever has happened in your daily life, find time to repair it at night. If it happens at night, you can use the daytime to repair yourself. Keep restoring your balance all the time. This is important.

Do you have any questions?

Q: Do dreams balance our waking life? I feel the dreams balance me.

Master Ni: Dreams do not balance your life. A dream can reflect reality. One part of your reality is that you have unclear dreams. The other part of reality is that you may see visions in dreams. By the information you gather from both, after correct interpretation, you can decide what you need to work on, whether from the clear reflection of your mind or your unclear dreams.

Dreams are pictures that you develop to show yourself the process of your life. They are like shadows. In other words, the dreams are as follows: a camera has taken a picture of reality. The dream is the developing process. However, the dream is only a reflection of the reality, it is not reality itself. That reality is more important than the dream.

Sometimes when something difficult happens in your life, you dream about it. Sometimes dreams can tell you the truth about something that you are not willing to face in life. Sometimes a dream is a vision. Your spiritual cultivation

can help you understand a dream so that you can sometimes foresee things and possibly avoid making a mistake.

*Q: Last time you talked about the "cats." I have a question
about that. How do you know when you are going to die?
It seems that I have nothing but dead cats around me. Can
you say something more about that. I recognize a dead cat.*

*Q: He wants to know how he can recognize the things in his
life that are like psychological dead cats.*

Master Ni: Let me start by telling all of you the story about
the dead cat, because some of you were not here last week.
When I was young and traveled around a lot, kind people
sometimes offered me food and lodging. One time, I stayed
for a few days with a family. The young daughter of the old
lord had a cat which was her companion when she did
embroidery or read poems in her room. The cat was almost
always there, quietly sitting by her side. The girl had a most
enjoyable youth, but she was over-protected by her parents.
Unfortunately, one day, the cat died for unknown causes.
Because the girl possessed a whole lot of poetic sentimentality, she was terribly sad about the death of the cat. She did
not even let the dead cat be removed from her side. For
days, she emotionally held onto the dead cat. Her holding
onto something that was no longer important or alive made
a deep impression on me as being unreasonable or unnecessary. I know many people who waste time in their lives by
doing that same thing emotionally.
    Since then, I use the term "dead cat" to describe bad
emotions, bad thoughts, bad memories, bad social or
political systems, religious prejudice and unreasonable
discrimination. People hold onto these unnecessary things.
People do not let them go. This causes an unhealthy reality
for themselves and the people who are around them.
    Your question is interesting. There are two ways to
react. One is if a young boy is mad at his parents who
refuse to allow him to do what he wants to do. Another is
if a parent sometimes disciplines a daughter, and she does
not listen. Then there is resentment. The boy and the girl

do not see that before they reach maturity, they need discipline. Later, when a person is mature, he or she understands. Like now, if I write a prescription for bitter herb tea for my patients, or do acupuncture on them, they accept readily because they understand it is to save them from a big problem. Thus, you need to be open to let your emotion to be guided by your rationality and accept willingly what your emotion might refuse. In all three cases above, an unpleasant experience happens to help or guide the person. Remember that the unpleasant experiences in one's life can help positive growth sometimes even more than the happy ones. No matter how bitter, help from any source can be beneficial. One only has to be open and use the opportunity to help oneself.

Practically, I think all of you know what I mean. Something that is already over, but the pain remains, is your dead cat, such as a broken heart experience. The pain still exists, but the thing is past. Now you can give up the dead cat and refresh your life and your spirit. Bring new hope and new strength into your life by looking to see what is the next good thing coming into your life. Sometimes you do things wrong, sometimes you might mistreat yourself. These are also 'dead cats,' including the resistance to spiritual development.

Once a great master was sitting in meditation. This was before he had achieved himself, when he was a beginner. Whenever he sat down to meditate, to calm his mind and to guide his own energy, he thought about the last moment of his life being like a dead cat. He just kind of threw it away and looked for the new life in this new moment. He did this for years in order to renew himself all the time. It greatly helped his achievement.

I mentioned the dead cat to the class because sometimes people are unsatisfied in life. I hoped to guide you to examine what you do with your energy. Those of you who are truly looking for growth may have seen that it is easy to have dead cats everywhere in your life if you are not careful.

Now, to answer your question, what do you do if everywhere in your life, all you see is your dead cats? Practically, you need to manage your life and learn to put it under your control in many areas, such as your finances and everything related to you. This may help eliminate some trouble-mindedness or dead cats. You know, sometimes eliminating dead cats is as simple a thing as cleaning out your closets. Look to see what is no longer alive in your life and see how you can better connect to this new situation you are in.

Also, in your relationships, maybe unhappy things happen, and you are troubled. If you are troubled, it is because there are two things you have not been doing. One is, you have not objectively looked at yourself. It means that your partner did not necessarily feel comfortable being with you, so he left. Or it could be out of many other reasons; make no mistake, a lot of what happens in relationships may have external or past causes. But if the person leaves, and if you keep the feeling of hurt in your mind, you are being unreasonable. Instead, go on to the next interesting thing in life to do.

Some people who have physical trouble, maybe small trouble, will misuse the money they have and go to a hospital to check it out. Sometimes they will go over and over again. Some doctors do not even understand internal causes; they check you out, examine you, give you lots of treatment and then hand you a big bill. All this helps you not one bit, but creates lots of disturbance, not only to your mind but to your body. The culture and medical technology of society has not developed that highly, but people trust it. Once they trust it, they bring more trouble to themselves. People do not know, "Your life is your responsibility." You should not use the power of money to take care of your own life. Take care of it yourself. Money can only help try to fix a problem that has already occurred. But you, by yourself, can keep problems from happening. Health is conditioned by diet and eating habits, emotion, lifestyle, the books you read and the friends you keep, etc. It is conditioned by your lifestyle and environment and thus it can be changed. If you work on these five terms as I pointed out, you do not need to rely on chemical, mechanical and technological medicine which cannot give you the service you can offer to yourself. External measures sometimes give you negative shadows by causing you to have different worries and more tension. They are not worth your total reliance.

The dead cat could be your own spiritual undevelopment. Throw it away and work to achieve clarity of mind. By this, you will be a happy cat, not a dead cat.

Q: You started out saying that people seek partners out of loneliness. And if they are not balanced, people will seek partners to prop them up. And if the partners leave them, they will fall down. Don't people seek partners out of health? Isn't it normal and healthy to have regular affection?

Master Ni: Surely, a healthy person with a balanced mind would like to have a partner. But only if that potential partner is suitable and fits well with one's practical life. It is good to get to know somebody a little, then keep yourself open to being able to decide whether to go forward or retreat. However, if someone with an imbalanced mind is looking for a partner, he or she might rush into a commitment without leaving room to retreat or for the other person to retreat if things are not working. Imbalance creates a demand that conditions future problems. This was what I meant.

A young daughter told her old father that she needed to go out. The father told her that it was already 11:00 p.m., but the daughter insisted, "I need to go out." The daughter thought her wish was healthy. The father had much concern about her. She thought, Why should I restrain myself? On the one hand, she was physically young and healthy and needed to find a mate. The father had more wisdom, a more achieved mind, and so he could see the two sides of the situation. It was not a matter of her going out; it was a matter of her going out under the right circumstances.

Similarly, with finding a mate or a partner, it is not a matter of doing it, it is a matter of doing it correctly. First of all, one needs to find the right partner. People have different destinies, but not everyone has the external or internal knowledge to be able to tell if a partner has a destiny that is compatible with his own. Everybody has a different energy formulation. At least, you can consider the moral condition of the other person.

Destiny is an interesting topic. When you observe people objectively, you may notice that some unattractive women get faithful husbands, and some ordinary men have attractive wives. Things do not always seem to match externally. This is because the pattern of life, or each individual's energy formation, allows a compatible match between the two.

Let us go back to the concept of a broken heart. If relationships do not seem to work for some people, it may well be that marriage is not in their destiny. They may have taken physical form to learn about something else this lifetime. Maybe they need to learn independence. Such person's may concentrate on and do well in their profession, mental development, spiritual development or social position. Once you know your energy and what kind of nature, lifestyle or life path you fall into, you can be a little more objective and less emotional about the good points of your situation. You become more realistic and thus happier. You do not need to go out at midnight to look for a husband.

If you struggle for a man but your energy formation does not support it, you will only bring unhappiness to yourself. It is more essential to attain your development. Once you know your limitations, it is better to stop searching in the dead alley and renew your main life path. In that way, you will find happiness, better than if you keep looking for what you cannot have in the first place.

If it is your destiny to have a certain relationship, that person will find you. It does not matter whether you are locked up in a nun's closet somewhere; that person will show up knocking on your door. So there is no point in agonizing over finding a relationship. Just go about your business, and keep open to the obvious.

So now let us say that you are over your broken heart and ready to try again. This time, be more careful. Pick your partner carefully. So many of today's people abuse sexual activity and are not responsible. You would not like to have AIDS or VD, or meet people who will influence you badly by taking drugs, etc. It is normal to have sexual activity, but only where and when you can find the right partner.

You are normal, but when people meet you, or when you meet people who come along, sometimes they may not be normal, so be careful. Try to use this method I teach you positively on different occasions to make yourself happy.

If you do not find the right person, I have given you the exercises of Eight Treasures and T'ai Chi movement to keep yourself internally satisfied. Taoist spiritual practice follows the principle of internal intercourse to complete your energy. It brings one part of the energy to meet and harmonize with other part of your own energy. This is the harmony of yin and yang. Not only does it express harmony and balance in your life, but it also provides further spiritual integration. I repeat: These exercises bring the two parts of your energy, yin and yang, to intercourse with each other. That will help you express harmony and maintain balance in your life. It will also provide further spiritual growth.

These are beautiful techniques and useful methods that we provide for you to have a complete life no matter what happens. A Taoist may not have a wife, but everything he enjoys could be like a wife to him. His work and his hobbies can be his wife. If his heart was broken, he can thus transform his sadness into happiness.

Before you develop yourself, if you have a broken heart, and you have self-pity, it is because your mind is small, and your heart can only hold one person or embrace one person. A Taoist's mind is so huge, it can embrace the entire universe. This is called developing an open mind. The whole universe is life; how can a person be disappointed in the heart, or feel loneliness?

I have set up three goals for the fundamental measurement of Taoist practice. In Taoist practice, first make your body light and pleasant. Do you feel that your body is light and pleasant? If you do not, then what is the trouble? First you need to do the Taoist exercises and practices. After doing the exercises, check yourself out: Do you feel you are light and pleasant? If yes, then you are approaching the first goal. Do not worry, however, if you do not reach that goal during the first months of practicing the exercises. It takes longer for some people than for others.

Second, how is your emotion? Is it happy, calm and quiet? If something makes you happy, then you are emotionally excited. The excited feeling will last for one moment; then it will go away and you will feel depressed again. However, the happiness you feel from doing the Taoist practices is not emotional excitement. It is quiet and internal, so beautiful. You enjoy it. You can ask my students who do T'ai Chi movement or Eight Treasures how they feel after doing the exercises. Do they feel excited like a wild person? No. They feel happy. They feel quiet too, because they enjoy themselves. Above all, they like themselves.

The third condition regards the mind. After doing the Taoist practice, the mind is enlightened. The mind becomes calm and clear. Enlightenment sometimes means having a special experience, which can be useful. But in everyday life, enlightened means meeting situations with calmness and clarity. You need to be calm, centered and clear when you are doing your business, when you contact people and face the world. If you lose clarity, what happens? You pay too much for something or someone takes advantage of you.

In Taoist learning, intellectual understanding is important. So are the practices. They help your mind become calm and clear. When that happens, then your spirit will be firm and unshaken by circumstance.

If you take root in your spirit, you become unshakable. If you live on the surface of things and events, you are vulnerable. In some people's daily life, when a little trouble happens, they are shaken and they yell, "My goodness, I do not know how to handle this." Some of you are so easily shaken. No, you cannot be that way. So if you follow my practices, you become more firm, unshakable and strong.

Being spiritually strong is not being physically or emotionally strong. Physical or emotional strength sometimes expresses itself as aggression. To be spiritually strong means to be centered within yourself so that you are calm. You have everything, because spirit contains all opportunity of life. It diminishes or destroys the necessity for death. So I recommend it to you.[2]

In the ancient time, the naturally spiritually developed masters developed the practices to serve you. Now is the time to learn the skills to make you a happy person, who will not suffer from a broken heart.

After you clear up your broken heart, I would like you to help me to develop the understanding of the Integral Truth and teach the practices to other friends and society. Today's society needs lots of help. So it is time to purify one's life and help human society have a healthy life. Open yourself, and do not think about the pain of your personal small trouble. Instead, we can work together and be spiritual friends with all. As the world learns more, every man and woman will be healthy and have a sound mind.

What I have taught you are the treasures the ancient developed ones handed down to us. If you do not use them, you are like a rich beggar; in your pocket you have a lot of cash, but you forget to use it and are standing on the street corner, begging for pennies. The cash in your pocket is your handy spiritual cash. So do your spiritual cultivation when sitting, standing, moving, walking and lying down. All opportunities given to you in life are for your spiritual development. All the methods and practices can help you develop. You can learn them all, but choose the best ones to keep practicing.

Keep working on your understanding. You can always find your answer in my books if you have a little patience. Or discuss your questions with other students in the class.

1985, Malibu Shrine

---

[2]*The practices are given in different books by Master Ni.- Editor*

Chapter 2

Smooth Your Emotions

Part 1

Q: What is your advice for when an emotional difficulty is experienced?

Master Ni: In this moment, I offer this suggestion that may have some spiritual meaning. I am about to introduce to you a Taoist principle of how to handle one's emotions, especially in a family or with the people who live with you under the same roof. As you become a person of wisdom, this principle is not only used with the people who are close to you. You sometimes need to use it with people who live under the same sky with you. Your depth and width cover all people like the sky. That is the personality that is the Taoist's pursuit.

In Taoist learning and teaching, we like to build the mind and heart to have depth like a mountain valley. This is termed having "deep-valley heartedness" or "deep-valley mindedness." Emotion is just the vapor or fog that comes to lay on the outer part of the human structure or on the surface of the valley. This means the emotional level is shallow. We do not encourage the use of emotion to disturb the deep heart or deep mind.

Above the surface of the sea, there are wind and waves. They can be strong and vicious. However, the conditions of the surface of the sea are not the same as in the depth of the water. The ocean floor is also a valley. This is another description Taoist culture values and calls "ocean-deep mindedness" or "ocean-deep heartedness." They can be obtained by your spiritual cultivation and meditation. Practically, it is one goal of your spiritual achievement.

How can you have "deep-valley heartedness" or "ocean-deep mindedness"? Like this: Although you have a fully sensitive spirit and sensitive mind, you can make a choice about how you react to things. You can react to the sting or bite of an ant without it involving your whole life being.

However, when it comes to the degree or intensity of their emotions, many people react to an tiny ant bite as though they had poison ivy from head to foot.

It is common to overreact to things that are not meaningful or valuable to your life. Frequently your emotion has already been brought to the surface by the tension of your work or just by living in a highly nervous society. These factors cause people to build a habit of over-reacting to a matter. That overreaction can be out of heavy emotion.

Spiritual cultivation builds up your deep and clear vision which enables you to see how important any matter is. You understand what different responses will cost you in terms of time, trouble or dignity. Then after you have the correct understanding, you react.

Another important Taoist teaching for dealing with your emotion is not to be attached to whatever is in front of you. This attitude of detachment can help you maintain objectivity. As long as you have objectivity, you still have room in your mental capacity to choose how to react to a situation. Or you can choose not to react to a situation at all. Detachment does not means not caring about a situation or person; it means giving the situation or person a little space when they need it.

The secret of cooperating in a Taoist family is to appear somewhat like an "emotional simpleton." In Taoist emotional life, being an "emotional simpleton" is a high spiritual achievement. By "emotional simpleton" I am describing a person who is slow to react emotionally. This person does not quickly come forward with an emotional response, but might mull a matter over before responding in a certain way. Or the person simply responds without putting any emotion at all in the response. If you would like to have objectivity and transcendence, you can learn the power of not reacting to a matter in an emotional way. Or you learn to slow yourself down enough so that you have time to respond in a way that will benefit the situation rather than be an impulse for which you will have to apologize later.

When you slow yourself down, your response to your family or beloved one will not be sharp or hurtful. I am unhappy when I see situation-comedy shows on television.

The characters appear to make witty comments or seem to look clever or sharp, but in real life, that kind of sarcasm and pointedness is damaging to others. Unfortunately, many people try to imitate what they see on television. If you speak that way to your parents or loved ones, your sharpness will hurt them and a new trouble will come back to hurt yourself. I mean, your comment will trigger an emotional response from them.

Once I was giving advice to someone who had emotional trouble with family members. I told him that in such a situation, you should not hurt somebody related to you, because family relationships are natural and respectful. Unless the utmost tact is used, the family will fall apart. Family relationships or emotions can be volatile because family members know each other so well. So most of the time, when one of your family members says something that seems like an attack, learn to be an "emotional simpleton." If you react with equal or sharper emotion or equal attack, there will be a big war and much destruction will take place in your personal life.

At first the person agreed with me, but a few minutes later, he had a thought. He said, "Master Ni, if your 14-year old daughter has a date with a boyfriend and it is almost midnight and she is still not home, can you be an 'emotional simpleton'?"

When there is responsibility, sometimes emotion is necessary. You have responsibility to discipline your daughter or son. This is spiritual responsibility. You cannot pretend to be a simpleton in such a circumstance. Being an "emotional simpleton" is not a medicine that will cure all. First, you need to fulfill your spiritual responsibility. Sometimes, being a simpleton and not reacting to an emotional attack is one way of fulfilling your spiritual responsibility.

This and any technique learned from me or my books must be put to proper application. I can give the technique and some suggestions. How to apply a technique correctly in your own life can be learned only by you. There is a different spiritual responsibility and fulfillment. I mentioned this, because I wish you do not mix up my teaching by applying it to the wrong situation. It is your responsibility.

In the situation of the teenage daughter, you can perhaps still use the skill of being an "emotional simpleton." How you respond depends on how you apply yourself. Youngsters need help to prepare their lives. Give them important advice in different opportunities before any difficulty happens. It is hard for them to accept a helpful punishment even if you did explain right and wrong and how you would like them to learn discipline from you. Before your daughter comes home, you have time to straighten out your thinking so that she does not receive an emotional shower. Instead, she receives correct and unemotional punishment that fits the wrongdoing. Also, you can explain to her clearly, firmly but unemotionally, why her behavior was wrong so her understanding will be clear. Then she will learn.

Set up guidelines in advance to meet certain circumstances. For example, the family should have a policy of calling whenever anyone is late. If this had been established, the daughter would have remembered to call home. Also, with such a young girl, the date could have been arranged in advance so that the father knew exactly where his daughter was during the whole evening and could call there. Explanations of the reasons or principles behind the guidelines will be instructive to youngsters and assist with their good self-management. All good habits can be formed when young. It is a responsibility and contribution to young life. Most of all, make a good example of your own life. Otherwise, if you say you love your children, this kind of love has no reality.

The skill of being an "emotional simpleton" gives you some room to organize a useful response. Most of the time, you do not need to react to another person's emotion at all. Being an "emotional simpleton" is not to be applied only when it suits you or is to your advantage. I mean that you make this type of consideration a part of your personality for the betterment of the relationship, not just for your personal gain. You can do it to benefit the other person, too, and at the same time practice your spiritual virtue.

Those who learn to be "emotional simpletons" are blessed. They are immune to pain and being wounded in many circumstances, because the situation will correct itself. Being such a wise simpleton, the sweetness produced by your forgiveness for another's offence and the secret kindness you give to the ignorant is a way to save trouble.

An "emotional simpleton" is not sensitive to unimportant things. An "emotional simpleton" does not know how to complain about unimportant details and does not remember what minor trouble people have caused. By learning this small skill of being an "emotional simpleton" and applying it in the correct instance, you will have the entire world for your spiritual joy, privacy and cultivation.

I do not have much to offer for advice on emotional matters. Most of the time you cannot stop the arguments in your surroundings. Yet you can learn to be an "emotional simpleton" to save the level of meaningless involvement. You also save the great waste of losing energy in unnecessary disputes and fights. Otherwise, you do not have time or energy to do anything better than that.

By nature, people who are less physical are more sentimental. Sentimentality has a high value in literature and drama, but in your own life, it poisons your overall health. Learning to be an "emotional simpleton" is a high achievement that takes some practice.

On the spiritual level, there is no difference between what is called high and what is called low, what is called easy and what is called difficult. The simpleton is wise. The highest thing is the lowest thing. The easiest task is the most difficult task.

You will face many emotional challenges during your lifetime. If you choose to be an "emotional simpleton," you can stand on the shore of dry land and be saved from the vicious wave attack of the emotional ocean. In other words, being an "emotional simpleton" can save you from emotional challenges. However, the one who sometimes does not choose to respond to a challenge would look foolish, but he is wise. Often, the one who looks smart suffers by a too quick response to the situation. This person may be perceived by other people as rude, arrogant or simply being out of place. This all causes personal emotional bitterness later.

It is hard to define what learning to be spiritual means. It sounds like I am saying that to be spiritual, you need to learn to be a simpleton. What I am saying is that to preserve the peace that is necessary for your survival, your happiness or to further your spiritual cultivation, learn to cope well with situations and respond correctly. In this contribution from the tradition of Tao, spiritual integrity and wholeness will follow after you reach clarity of emotion.

Part 2

In order to attain inner clarity and freedom of the soul, you have to get your emotions under control. In general, we can hardly define who has a high moral quality or a low moral quality. There are important factors that decide each individual's spiritual future. It is improvement and refinement brought about in each individual's spiritual cultivation that determine an individual's spiritual future. It seems that spiritual achievement itself is not a great obstacle, once you understand what is helpful and what is not. What is left for most people is their own emotions, which affect the way they treat themselves and others. This will cause trouble for themselves or for other people.

Sometimes you overreact to a small irritation and so forth, or you over defend your mistake or wrongdoing. Traditionally there are techniques to help one's emotional trouble, but I was not particularly interested in the subject. When you are younger, you sometimes deny emotion. You get over things quickly. You just feel interested in going around everywhere to look at things and play. Your sisters may henpeck you. Your brother may snoop on you and report everything to your parents. You usually can escape the discipline of your parents. However, you seldom have a sharp emotional reaction to a thing; you just know to enjoy yourself. You do not have a problem on this level. But you may be warned that when you grow stronger, also your emotion will grow stronger too. Your confidence will grow stronger. Your stronger confidence will bring about an equally stronger emotion towards the world. When your confidence is less strong, the emotion is less strong, and when the outside world comes to attack you, you are more receptive. When you are strong, you try to fight back, counterattack, then a small issue becomes a big emotion. You make a small emotion into a big emotion.

The matter of emotions is like the water in Long River which starts in the west of China, Tibet and Chinghai, goes through Szechuan province and ends at the sea. The water gathering together becomes a strong flow and goes all the way down. It is dangerous for a boat to travel on the river, especially in some spots. You do not see the danger ahead, but in some places, under the smooth surface of the water, is a turbulence like a whirlpool.

The emotional flow is exactly like the flow of water. If underneath the smooth surface of the river there are stones or holes, they will make the water become turbulent. Similarly, if under the smooth surface of a person's exterior there are rough or unrefined places, they will make the person's emotion become turbulent. Just as the pattern or the flow of the water in a stream down a mountain is determined by the lowest place available for the water to flow, your emotional reactions are determined by whatever is low within yourself. Your reaction is different at different times because your general psychological condition changes all the time during your everyday life.

When you are in a good mood or your energy is high, whatever people kid you about or tease you about, you handle it well. Even if you feel something will threaten or endanger you, you are still calm. If your mood is bad or your energy is low, or if any thoughts are already underlying your psychological condition, then your emotional reaction will be much worse than if you are in a normal mood.

So there are levels of depth. First always check out what is underlying your psychology. Is there anything that has made you frustrated? Anything that made you feel set back? Anything bothering you? If so, in the situation coming upon you, do not react. If you react, your reaction will not be appropriate. Instead, it will reflect your inner workings. Your energy is tied up internally in trying to resolve a conflict or make a decision, and your reaction will come from that. Then how do you solve the frustration?

Women have physiological cycles. When the cycle is low, during menstruation or ovulation, they react to things more slowly because their energy is tied up internally in the bodily process. People interpret this slowness as a bad mood or will think the woman is unhelpful.

In any situation in life, if we are more peaceful, then we will not make it more colorful, more stimulating or more disturbing than it really is. Sometimes a situation can even become destructive to people. Surely, whatever you do towards people, you also do towards yourself too.

Of the two types of emotion defined by the ancients, one is fiery; it is explosive and burning like a volcano. It begins abruptly and finishes soon, to become all ashes. How can the nervous system of the human body take that? If you understand that, you will know that being spiritual is not different from emotional control.

Because you are spiritual, the biggest trouble is that you have lack of emotional control. You are not yourself. You are in the water, but you do not know how to manage sailing your boat correctly.

Historically, when China was under a system of monarchy, all injustice would be created by that system. A monarch is powerful enough to destroy other people. He can kill his ministers or advisers if he wishes. But at the same time, he can equally cause the loss of his empire by an emotional mistake. Sometimes a king loses his kingdom for loving a woman. Emotion can also cause one to lose vision or ignore the responsibility of furthering a peaceful world.

Sometimes a monarch or leader builds a preference and only listens to advice from a certain group of people. If he does not like provocative advice and cannot listen in a balanced way to all advice, he cannot put all the sides together to find the right thing to do. This is how sometimes monarchs kill or fire good, valuable and loyal people who help them by accurately reflecting reality, even if it is not pleasant. Some monarchs would rather keep people who please them while undermining their throne.

Each person has his own throne. Who undermines yours? It is still yourself. A woman is queen-like when she is a person of self respect. Women are "queens" and men are "kings," and they can stay on the "royal throne" if they do not make trouble for themselves by establishing a preference or a fondness for something. Preference leads to uncontrolled emotion, which becomes costly. Preference, fondness and emotion become a burden, then you lose balance.

Spiritual traditions hardly ever talk about emotion, because they are already over that stage. When you are emotional, you lose the vision to see things clearly. You cannot control your tongue and might say something that would destroy the beautiful picture of your life.

The difficulty of being spiritual is not because you are not moral enough, or you are not spiritual enough, but because you are captive to your emotions. It is important to know that. It can be overcome. If you overcome 70% of your emotional problem, you are already above average people, and you are happy and light like a bird.

Spiritual cultivation requires devotion, spiritual learning and a spiritual path. We need to devote ourselves to the teaching of the ancient teachers and sages. We are students; we cannot say we are already perfect. What the teachers and sages teach is not for themselves; they are helping us. To learn their teaching takes devotion. If you have that devotion, you will already have your emotions controlled. At least you already keep the fox or wolf leashed or caged. Then you can get along well with people and with yourself and slowly improve yourself. If you do not know how to get along with yourself, then surely you do not know how to get along with the world either.

So first have spiritual devotion in your spiritual learning. It is not to say you worship god and god will help you. You have to have your own spiritual devotion that can help you. Mostly, it is not conceptual, it means the devotion to the real guidance, real teaching which can build you up spiritually. That is important. First you have devotion, then you use it to level your emotion.

A calm person is seldom annoyed by his family or the world. He has emotional reactions; surely he reacts because he is alive. But it is soon over; he never allows the clouds to cover his shining spiritual sun. If you allow your emotion to develop, every day will be a cloudy day because you cover the spiritual sun which radiates the light of wisdom. What can you do about it? A wise person is a decisive and determined mind. He or she has the least emotions. Most people talk about their emotion and their preferences. They are always pushing their emotions to opposite extremes in order to gain real benefit or achievement. In a certain stage at least, they lose their happiness during those occasions.

So first we have devotion. Second, for our psychological and emotional health, we do spiritual practice which really helps us: some good hymns, a little good chanting, a little meditation, a little useful invocation, a little recitation of a good poem or spiritual passage, anything helpful will do. Just get your monkey mind under control. Do not let the monkey out to destroy the good fruit in your life tree. The monkey picks up the fruit from your life tree and wastes it. If you use the *Workbook for Spiritual Development for all People*, you will receive the bonus of good emotional conduct plus spiritual development.

What is our physical reaction when emotion comes? Some breathing techniques can be learned. When you are young, your emotional problem is small if you do not exaggerate it. When you are older, bigger, your emotion will grow. Weaker emotional force causes fewer problems than strong emotion. Even when a problem is bigger than you can handle, if you cannot handle your emotion, you cannot control the problem, but the problem will easily defeat you. It is like dancing on a slippery wet stone; you will not be able to stand well by yourself.

In your life, you cannot count on forgiveness or mercy from other people. You always need to guide yourself to step firmly in the right place or right position.

This would be your own experience: When you are young, you do not have unhealthy emotion. You are a child who enjoys all the time; you eat well and sleep well, and so you enjoy whatever comes to your hand. This teaching is not to help you there, but when you are older and you live in the world, and you are not protected, when you need to extend your protection to others, you will have emotional experiences. When you do, you need to be ready to handle them. You need to overcome your emotion, not let your emotion overcome you. You need to be triumphant over your emotion, not let your emotion triumph over you.

When you are older, especially when you live in the world, you see many people. Sometimes they kill each other or even themselves because of emotions such as revenge or craziness. To judge a person correctly is not an easy job, before a person is expressed by his behavior. There is no accurate way to put the person on the scale to judge his morality or spirituality. However, even a good person may do something strange, the result of which he may not be capable of controlling. Definitely such a person is enslaved or captured by his emotions. All these actions occur from violent emotion.

A spiritually responsible person always knows to discipline himself instead of attacking other people.

The next part is Taoist guidance. Let us say that you have devotion in spiritual learning and also do your cultivation regularly. If emotion happens, and it is too big for you to handle, it will create pressure inside your body. I need to give you some techniques. If you learn them, you still need to improve yourself constantly without establishing self indulgence or self pity and looking for people's forgiveness. If you indulge in self pity, my teaching will not help you; how can you wish to be a useful person in the world?

Nobody can afford to be useless. You can be useless to people of evil leadership, but you still need to be useful in your personal life to the real good natural life.

Part 3

You grow to know that men and women both need most of all to guide themselves away from emotion. There are two types of emotion. One type excites you and another dismays you. The physiological reaction to the two types of common situations, excitement or dismay, creates different internal detrimental pressures. It causes organs to have problems. The organs which are affected by your emotions are your heart, liver and female organs. They all react to your emotion. For example, anger is a form of excitement which causes the vapor inside of the body to press the heart and liver. Thus, sometimes holding anger or emotion inside will cause a liver or heart problem. That is often seen, but general people and general medicine do not understand the connection between emotion and the organs.

If people have a worry or are emotionally low, it causes stagnation inside. That will usually cause trouble for the stomach or lower organs, and will also become a physical problem. There are also external problems, such as overeating or inferior practices like using drugs or mechanical things in sex or masturbation. These can all cause trouble.

Now I am specifically talking about emotion. Two types of breathing can help you release the pressure you have created by yourself. The Eight Treasures, T'ai Chi movement or Ba Gua movement can give general help. You can help your whole being by exercise which will conduct and release your internal pressure to change the condition and balance your life being. It will have a helpful effect upon you if you do it correctly and consistently.

Now I would like to mention something specific in case you do not have a chance or you do not like to learn the Eight Treasures or other Taoist physical arts. Or if you have already learned them, but you still wish to learn a technique in case you do not have a chance to practice. Those exercises are for general care. Now I am talking about a specific treatment to help you. First, see what kind of emotion affects you, then treat it by this practice.

The first type is when excitement such as anger makes the energy vapor rise. This causes tension and pressure in the upper body. Go to look for an open space, or even better, face an evergreen tree or bushes. Bushes are better than trees for this purpose, because they are lower than your height. Your vision should not rest upon anything higher than you, so look for something on the ground much lower than you. Then you inhale and poof out the breath.

You make noise like a loud exhale, either gently or vigorously, depending on how badly you are congested in the upper part of your body. Do it five times. If the trouble is much bigger, do it maybe thirty-six times. Then it will be all gone, no more congestion.

Sometimes a stagnancy or congestion in the lower body is caused by worry, too much thought, or oversleeping, all of which can cause you to be somewhat deflated, just like a tire. In that case, your physical function slows down. Maybe you can sit in a chair, or put a chair outdoors and look up in the sky or at the top of a tree. Be sure to look at something that is taller than you are or over your head. Inhale and hold the breath, then gently release it either with or without sound. The point is to hold the breath. Holding the breath keeps the pressure in the upper body. Then release the breath. Because worry or vexation is usually chronic, it takes a longer time to accomplish the balancing.

After doing this practice from five to twenty-four times, start to do the practice for general enhancement of breathing. Slowly count one, two, three. Inhale on one inhale, hold the breath on two and exhale on three. Inhale, hold, exhale. Inhale, hold, exhale. Do this between thirty-six and eighty-one times. The meditation can be from fifteen to thirty minutes; then you will be enhanced internally.

This practice for general enhancement of breathing can also help you enhance your vitality. The other two, as I described at the beginning, help your emotion. Often a women's nervous system is more sensitive; she reacts more, so this will help her. This is applicable to all people, whether man or woman.

Sometimes the biggest problem is that you react to trouble too fast. If you react to a problem too fast, you know that immediately you have to make an excuse to go away to do the practice. Do not come back to face the same emotion again, but give yourself a half day or several hours, then come back to face the emotion. This is much easier.

The emotional level is a much lower level than the normal mind, which is the foundation of an active spirit. Emotion is a more external level. Emotion will not hurt your soul, but it will hurt your physical health, which then affects your internal energy. Learn to help yourself and adjust your emotion by breathing. Emotion directly changes your breathing pattern, circulation and secretions. By practicing breathing, you change your circulation and secretion so you are not affected by your response to the world.

One good way to conduct your emotion is with beneficial music. Taoist gentle music is especially good; it consists of the music from different natural instruments such as fiddles, made from wood or bamboo. The melody is mostly an imitation of natural voice such as water flowing in a stream, birds chirping in the trees, a gentle wind blowing over a meadow, white clouds wandering across the sky freely, and gentle waves on a lake, etc. This peaceful music does not only conduct your emotion, it also has a healing power for chronic problems, or at least gives some assistance. I make it available in cassette tapes. It will be useful for you too.

Chapter 3

Harmony is the Product
Of Spiritual Cultivation

People are born with different temperaments. Those differences in temperament can even be seen in the Chinese birth chart of an individual. Practically, this shows that some women or men will not find happiness in marriage or friendship. This is because the temperament of the person unconsciously tends to be argumentative. Being argumentative leads to break-ups if the partner does not feel especially comfortable with arguments.

I have seen, for example, that if a woman is too argumentative, she will feel unsuitable as somebody's wife or partner. However, if such a personality is married to somebody who needs that kind of energy, and perhaps if the woman has more knowledge and the man has less knowledge, the woman can take the lead and maybe the situation can be turned around.

Once a visitor came from Europe and asked me to do a life consultation for her. I could immediately tell her that there was nothing wrong and that only one thing needed to be changed: she must stop being argumentative with her boyfriend. The point I make here is that one's temperament exists objectively. There is no need for self-complaint; the individual needs only to work to change herself. She admitted to that shortcoming and said that it was the reason that her boyfriend was hesitating about marriage and settling down together.

Marriage or a relationship requires spiritual cultivation. Most people have the same level of moral nature; nobody is lacking and nobody is excessive. Then basically, respect for each other can usually be found. Most people respect the same moral realization.

Unfortunately, some people tend to be more opinionated, more judgmental and more argumentative. If a person has that nature, and if it is not utilized in one's profession - as with a lawyer or a judge - and if this tendency or nature is applied to one's partner in everyday life, it becomes an unbearable element. So the best thing is to learn how to work around it. Unfortunately, people with that tendency usually look for somebody who is able to take it. If they cannot find someone like that, there will be no happy ending for them.

It is a precious achievement to change yourself to admit a personal problem and allow self-forgiveness. That is one way to fix yourself.

Some couples get along well because of financial stability and close educational background. Some areas of life are easier to work out; the difference in temperament is more difficult to work out. In a good match, one person's shortcoming is mended by the other person, and so each person can ignore the other's lack. The best situation is when a couple can complement each other's personalities, abilities, strengths and weaknesses. That makes things work even better.

There is self knowledge involved in having a happy life. First we need to define a "happy life." Human society developed its view or opinion about what is a happy life. Usually it means marriage and family and so forth. Is that a happy life? That standard is a social custom and does not include everybody. I do not reject nor support that standard. I believe that each individual has to have knowledge of his or her suitability to be a husband, wife, mother or father. If you discover that you are not suitable or not really interested, then you should not choose that path. A lot of people have a kind of strong internal contradiction around this question. On the one hand, you have your self-knowledge that it is not suitable for you to live that kind of life, but on the other hand, because of social pressures, you would like to. This kind of internal contradiction will cause all kinds of trouble and messiness in your life. It is not worth wasting your time on internal struggle. I still respect personal knowledge about whether a person is fit or not for a certain lifestyle.

Generally speaking, people have the spiritual capability to know if someone they have met is suitable to be their potential spouse or partner or not. Unfortunately, many things can pressure a person, like strong desire, loneliness or social influence, and some people end up making choices that cheat themselves. They say to themselves, "I want it, I need it, I love it," but they ignore the inner knowledge that tells them, in a deep sense, "This is not the right one."

Many people jump onto the bus or the ferry boat in a hurry without understanding their goal. Marriage or partnership is, of course, much more serious than taking a wrong bus or ferry boat. So now we come down to a key point in the consideration of marriage and partnership: it is not that people do not have self-knowledge, but that people practice self-deception. Because their physical desire or emotions are stronger and given more credence than their own self-knowledge, they ignore their own inner wisdom. They are reaching for a temporary solution or providing satisfaction for an emotional or physical need. It is often unavoidable that a partnership based on such a shaky foundation crumbles.

I do not suggest that you need to go to a fortune teller to find out if you should marry someone or not. Usually you are more accurate than any fortune teller. External reasons are not appropriate grounds for marriage. If you wish to solve the problem of this moment but you do not look at the problem of the next moment, what harmony can there be when there is such an underlying problem? Harmony can only be based on having no problem. That is, harmony is based on being spiritually centered. It does not mean that you do not have a problem; almost everyone has a problem. It means that you are not looking to the relationship as the solution to that problem. Such a desire usually will create illusion when you meet someone. If the relationship starts and reality fails to meet that fantasied expectation, unhappiness will result.

When there is harmony, temperamental adjustment is not a big obstacle. Mutual financial and emotional support can be given, but there are still differences between individuals because their childhoods, backgrounds and physical foundations are different. On that level of difference, harmony can be attained by developing understanding.

More important is loyalty to each other. Loyalty brings about mutual trust. Without mutual trust, you have doubt or suspicions about the other person. If you have that suspicion - it does not even need to be reality, only a mind already uneasy in the depths - then any superficial occurrence can cause an outburst, a fight or a breakup.

So what can you do to bring about a good relationship? First pick the right person for you. Then, work on being earnest; do you truly love your partner more than anybody else? No, you could not. Although there are lots of beautiful men and women out there, they are not your real opportunity. Even if temptation comes into your life, you still need, realistically speaking, to think about it. Would you really like to begin all over again with a whole new program? Once again, you would have to look for mutual trust, eliminate the suspicion or jealousy, see if you can emotionally help each other and so forth. A new situation is always a pending situation. It is not like the foundation of an old relationship, where everything is already worked out and you know everything about it.

If you kick out one partner to jump into a new opportunity, you may count yourself to be lucky if the new one is better than the old one. There are a few lucky people. If you discover that the new opportunity is worse than the last one, you will feel terrible. You will complain about yourself, put yourself down and undermine your own confidence. Maybe you will come close to a dangerous depression.

We are slowly getting around to the basic point. The basic point is personal growth. Life is not easy; life needs to be learned. Surely some people do not learn by their own experience; they marry five times and still cannot be happy with the new husband or wife. Maturity means you have observed all the kinds of marriage. Because you have grown up in a family, your first observation is the marriage of your father and mother. You learn about their problems. Basically, we all grew up in the same school; the teachers were different and the type of teaching was different, but practically we all observed clearly what was needed to be done and what was considered right or wrong, good or bad.

Men and women are not necessarily on the same level; sometimes women are more intelligent but more temperamental. This is generally speaking, and in some cases the opposite is true. It does not serve any individual when competition arises between the two. The better way and better idea is the one that can be accepted. Be careful about what I say here. Men and women cannot concentrate their demands on their partners. It means not to impose personal expectation and wish to shape one's partner according to one's own ideas. When a man marries a woman, he cannot demand that she has to be a wonderful cook, a wonderful lover, a wonderful dancer, a wonderful flower arranger and the best in housekeeping, etc. Forget it; nobody is perfect. I believe that she does her best. Neither can a woman put all concentration or pressure on a man, that he must be handsome, physically robust, have lots of money, have lots of vacation time to spend with her, provide everything needed, especially emotionally, and make her feel proud in society. Forget it; you cannot get everything from your husband.

Why sometimes do a husband and wife secretly complain about a bad marriage but still get along? It is not the problem of the reality of the marriage that they are complaining about; it is the problem of some dissatisfaction due to imaginary projections and hopes that were not fulfilled by the partner. In the world, there are lots of unfair things, but the most unfair is when a woman or a man has tremendous expectations of his or her partner and demands that the partner fulfill these emotional needs. For example, if a man is looking for beauty, he can buy a dummy that stands in the window of the department store; it is dressed beautifully. Unfortunately that dummy only looks beautiful and cannot do anything else. If he marries a human dummy like that, he will feel frustrated when his other needs are not met. If a woman thinks that on top of everything that he already does for her, she still needs that rich and handsome man to treat her as if she were a queen, to obey her and be faithful to her; she will run into the reality that it is really hard to find someone like that.

Although men and women establish the emotional pattern of looking for a complete and perfect man or woman, practically no such person exists. Every human being has shortcomings.

So what is marriage? It is having a certain maturity. You have to attain a certain maturity if you really wish to get the most from the marriage. Otherwise, you get nothing. A marriage is like jumping into the frying pan. Sometimes a man or a woman is not strong physically. A man and woman's cycles cannot always meet perfectly so that they can have sexual harmony all the time. We will talk about sexual harmony in another chapter. But the most important, the most fundamental thing is that you need good company. That is the primary consideration. If the basic partnership cannot be formed correctly, you will end up with too many troubles. Such a relationship is just like buying an old car; you do not know when it will fall apart on the road, but you know it will. The problems are underlying and everybody is waiting for something to happen.

Nobody is problem free when they enter a marriage. Marriage will not work unless the people accept that marriage is just that way. No matter what, there will be difficulties and some natural conflict. Marriage with a certain amount of conflict and difficulties still remains in the healthy category.

Q: What about people who try for years but just cannot get along, perhaps because their personalities or habit patterns are too different?

Master Ni: If there is a strong disagreement in life or in spirit, what is sometimes appropriate is for each to go their separate ways. A fresh beginning gives an opportunity for a person to renew himself or herself. There is no need to stay attached to and keep mulling over what the other person did or is doing. The most important thing is to keep your focus on your happy and creative life, and what you can do for others.

You know, sometimes after people separate, they keep a war or fight going internally for years by giving energy to thoughts about the failed marriage or trying to have the last word. They stay rivals even though they no longer see each other. The mature person gives up that type of behavior, even if the other one continues, and allows the contention to fade away. Some people never change or improve themselves, but that is not anyone else's responsibility nor is it cause for continued feelings of anger or regret.

Sometimes our "negative teachers", our unhappy experiences in life, give us the most impetus for our own spiritual growth and for moving us towards our positive good life.

Each person is an individual and learns in his or her own time. If a person cannot change, then all we can do is accept them for what they are and give our energy to positive expressions in our own life. No matter how much we have loved them, they can only be enlightened when they are ready for it. If they are no longer an element of your present life, then do not give further energy to your old frustration.

Q: You were talking about being argumentative and there is a big question about being argumentative and being able to discuss a matter.

Master Ni: That is important. If a husband and wife cannot be friends, but are only together for sexual need, the marriage cannot really be established. They must be friends first. Being friends means that the man likes to listen to the woman and vice versa. It does not mean you have to obey, but at least you listen to what is said. Both must be willing to discuss; then a friendship will exist. If there is no mutual mood for discussion, then with only one or two words there is the risk of an emotional fight. Small things turn into big things; the husband tries to pull the wife down and the wife tries to pull the husband down.

I once knew an unmarried couple that stayed together for six years. The man had some money and the woman had beauty and talent. The only matter that they could not settle was who should listen to whom and who would be in charge of the household. They could not resolve that question so they could not go into a marriage. In reality, they were not together psychologically; each of them was competing at being the boss. It is not possible to have two bossy people living in the same house, sharing the same room and sleeping in the same bed. Two people under one roof cannot both be the boss. Everything is open to discussion. Some things one person is good at, so he takes care of them. Some things the other person is good at, so she takes care of them. So there must be discussion. After they discuss a matter, whatever conclusion is arrived at must be appreciated by both sides. There is no "I am the boss," or "You are the boss."

In the small world of a couple, if there is external interference, many times friction will develop and become a real problem between them. I am not talking about an extramarital affair. I am talking about a friend, a family member or a mother-in-law, for example. When someone appears to take sides with one or other of the couple, it can create a small friction which turns into uncontrollable competition, rivalry and endless argument.

Anybody who is a guest under someone else's roof should always ignore, walk away from or avoid joining a disagreement between husband and wife, or any people living together. It is also wise not to invite family members to come and stay when a situation could be difficult or disturb the peace of the home environment.

To improve the texture of emotion after a small battle, quarrel or friction, if both parties are sensitive enough, they need to apologize for being offensive or bossy. Never build a habit of quarreling; each person needs to behave respectfully towards themselves and the partner.

Respect for the other person is what protects the continuity of love and tenderness in a relationship. Love and respect give enough space and room for the other person to make the adjustment to maintain the affection between them.

Q: So each person has his or her own domain and the other person respects the other one's domain and management of that department of life?

Master Ni: Generally speaking, women are competent in the kitchen or in the household, so why should the man always interfere? I think a man can learn to appreciate what a wife does for him. The woman can also appreciate the man cutting the firewood and doing what he does. In such a case, basic harmony exists and then we can talk about something else like having children. If the basic harmony does not exist, the relationship is just a kind of hitchhiking or ride which happens accidently, and there is no need to talk about anything deeper.

So discussion is important. It is important to appreciate what your partner says. Also, never call the other person stupid. Although you may be wiser, under the same roof nobody can be truly recognized as a sage. More importantly, there should not be two people playing "sage" under the same roof. When two people live together, it is better not to consider whatever wisdom you have achieved. The closeness of daily life and working together brings people down to the same level, even though one of them might have a better point of view. It is more like this: I show you my picture, you show me your picture, you see that part, I see that part, I agree with what you say, you agree with what I say, then we find a way out. We trust the knowledge from the one who has better knowledge on certain subjects.

A Chinese proverb says, even if you are a precise judge with clear vision, you cannot judge who is right and who is wrong between husband and wife. In the past, the sages did not dare talk about it. Because this area of life was a taboo, a forbidden area, a wise man did not touch it. It is now time to bring these important but forbidden subjects out into the bright sunshine so that people can look for inspiration.

Q: Are there any techniques that people can use in discussion or relationship to do well with each other?

Master Ni: It is not that people do not like discussion; what happens between two people is that their schedules are different and their energy cycles are different. If one person is tired and does not want to talk and the other person is in the mood to talk, this will cause an unsatisfying response. Sometimes one person is in a different mood and also cannot talk; so under the one roof there are different pots with different temperatures cooking on the stove. The temperatures need to be controlled.

I do not emphasize it, but a man and woman can prepare a segment of time each day or week to have a discussion. Usually the husband comes home tired from work, and if the wife stays home, she has lots of things she would like to tell the husband. The husband may not want to listen, so he sits in front of the TV to escape all communication. If their schedules are tight, it is better to set aside a dedicated time, like after a meal, when they can have a chance to sit together and discuss the day. Generally, the more informal the better, because that is life.

Each person's different cycles and moods can be seen. Whoever works inside the house needs to be more helpful and more serving. Discussion is still not the correct way to describe harmony, which is a kind of serving. The husband helps the wife in the kitchen work and the wife takes care of the husband who comes home from the outside. It is this little bit of gentle serving that makes communication beautiful and as sweet as lots of birds singing. There is no one law. True sincerity and true love, with clear observation, always finds space for different types of communication. Usually communication is nonverbal more than verbal and informal rather than formal.

We talked about moving a relationship towards the direction of harmony. There are a few things I would like to add. One is that the husband and wife, or partners, each need to have their own space or privacy. There needs to be some distance, because each person needs some room for self adjustments. Without some personal space for self adjustment, it is hard to live together. Also, it is not healthy for people to be too close; a healthy relationship has some personal space. I do not talk about how large a house to live in, but emotional space is needed so that each person can at least move around without being exposed to questioning all the time.

Each day, a person has a different climate. The climate is a natural matter; it changes back to normalcy by itself. A personal climate does not need external attention to change back to normal. It does not need questioning, adjusting or fixing. For one person to try to do so for another person is unskillful and causes the opposite response, stress. Therefore, this should be avoided. A man and a woman can respond to each other with simple words. They can also be sensitive enough to respect the other person's self-adjustment without interfering. This is the way to keep harmony.

The second thing is that, to prevent a broken heart, do not rely emotionally on the other person. If you create such a reliance, when one side pulls its energy back, even for a short while, you will fall. People in a relationship are usually constantly adjusting their energy, forward and back. Many tragic, unhappy, or disappointing love affairs are the result of one side giving too much imaginary love to another person. One might think that the other person is perfect and that no one else in the world can replace that person. If you decide that, it means you are going to be heartbroken when that person does not prove to be perfect or leaves. Rather, you must know that you can get along well with the same type of man or woman, not just that one person. Any two people who share similar life interests and daily habits are likely to get along well.

I am not saying you to be disloyal or disrespect your partner; only that it is most beneficial to have your own balance and be able to poise or contain yourself emotionally and mentally. Otherwise, without your own balance, you will have a crazy love, where you love so intensely that you lose your equilibrium and poise. Then if some external change happens, being overextended will make you fall and suffer. That can be avoided by your own spiritual cultivation and emotional discipline.

Third, you need calmly and realistically to understand the situation of your partner, such as the mood, the influence of the type of work the person does, etc.

Fourth, you need to have understanding. Sometimes a small thing, through one's own emotional exaggeration, can make a situation or relationship difficult. There are many things about the other person that are ultimately unimportant and that you can ignore. For example, you are a man and your wife or girlfriend is attractive. Just as you found her attractive, other men will also find her attractive. Sometimes she is skillful in turning them down. But sometimes she is not so skillful and in some way a little problem will catch up with her. You cannot be so jealous. Your own jealousy is your own problem. If you can just stay quiet, she will take care of her own problem. Some men are like that too. They need to resolve the little problems that catch up with them.

Each person is an individual. You cannot totally rely on another person to support you. Do not think, "You have become my spinal column." No way; you have your own spine.

The fifth circumstance is to be ready for change. Allow the situation to change, reasonably or unreasonably. What does that mean? It means, because you have attained objectivity, you can allow harmony to grow naturally. Harmony comes through allowing change. If you make everything organized and contracted, the harmony is artificial, not real. All experienced people know that any written contract is only as good as the hearts and intentions of the people who are involved in the cooperative endeavor.

So you let things change. You cannot be tyrannical and not allow change. If you allow only yourself to change, a good relationship cannot exist.

The ancient type of marriage was arranged by the parents. It was considered lucky when the couple got along well. In modern times, some couples do not get along well because they marry too young; they do not know themselves. That creates a situation needing more change and correction as the people come to understand themselves. If you have that understanding about yourself, you have your own harmony inside and that harmony will be expressed outside too. Things come from the inside and are then seen on the outside, as a good personality will bring about a good environment. It does not happen the other way around, that a good environment will bring about a good personality.

Therefore, if you wish external harmony only to foster internal harmony, it is usually a fantasy, and is not a real possibility.

It may sound like I am an expert in being a husband, but I am just an older person with some broad common-sense experience.

Many generations in China have considered Confucius to be a sage. In the Confucian dialogues there is a sentence that women do not like. He said that in the world, woman and children are hard to be with. It could be understood like this: it is a challenge to be with a woman and children. I believe you understand what Confucius meant. He was talking about no sageliness in his own household. I believe he had a hard time getting along with his wife and son and other relatives. I also believe sometimes a man can be like a spoiled child and thinks it is his partner that is difficult, while all the time it is him who is being difficult. I would say that under one roof, there is no one sage. So be careful. Never trying to be a sage is a sign of sageliness.

One more thing that needs to be added is that we always need to keep learning new things. Keep open to new things, small or big. It is important. Otherwise, life itself, and family life, becomes like a ditch filled with stagnant water. It will become corrupt. In your personality and in your personal life, adopt, accept and try new things.

If someone makes a constructive comment or suggestion, learn from it and adapt it into your life. Also, in a situation where two people have difficulty doing something together, try doing it in many different ways until you can achieve some success.

Chapter 4

Woman - the Mysterious Origin

This discussion is related both to women and men. In it, topics of relationship and emotion were discussed. Because people of both genders live in the world, this chapter has value for men readers. By doing so, perhaps both men and women can understand each other better.

The meeting begins by reading from the book, *The Complete Works of Lao Tzu*, Chapter 6:

The Subtle Essence of the universe is eternal.
It is like an unfailing fountain of life which
*   flows forever in the vast and profound valley.*
It is called the primal female, the Mysterious Origin.
The operation of the opening and closing
*   of the Subtle Gate of the Origin performs*
*   the Mystical Intercourse of the universe.*
The Mystical Intercourse brings forth all things
*   from the unseen sphere into the realm of the manifest.*
The Mystical Intercourse of yin and yang
*   is the root of universal life.*
Its creativity and effectiveness are boundless.

Master Ni: I welcome this meeting.

What I offer is advice for your spiritual cultivation. Please do not mistake me as a representative of men who comes here to talk to you. I represent the Tradition of Tao and its higher spiritual teachings, and have come to help you see if they have any relevance to your lives.

I hope that what I say here is not used as fuel to fire up arguments to prove that anyone is right or wrong, treated well or mistreated. You know, in human history, men and women (or even people of the same sex) have always argued among themselves about who was better, or who got better treatment, and people will probably always continue to argue these points. That is an unchangeable pattern of behavior at one level of human life.

That is one aspect of human life that is somewhat trivial. Each individual makes a personal choice about spending time or energy in argument.

Another aspect of human life that is perhaps more important and that is also relevant for women - and men - is equality in terms of social position or wages, and personal safety of the individual. It is interesting to see from a historical perspective that neither social equality or even safety can be planned or controlled by any leader, no matter if it is a political, social, spiritual or other leader. Thus the responsibility for one's safety and relationship with society lies with the individual.

Because these and other aspects of life relate to how you as an individual use your life energy, I suggest a spiritual approach to life rather than a political or social one. This is why I am here today. Because our focus is spiritual, this tradition can only advise you about individual spiritual cultivation and is not able to tell you how to run your life. You must work out the details of your life by yourself. It is each individual's choice, even when it comes to selecting what kind of guidance you are open to listening to and thinking about. Because spiritual principles apply equally to all individuals regardless of gender, whatever advice I give serves both men and women equally.

Let me see now, it looks as though you range in age from 25 to 50. Most of you are in your thirties. I am glad to see all of you and give you an opportunity to ask some questions about spirituality from the woman's point of view. Before we begin with the questions and answers, let us just chat a little while.

The Tradition of Tao from the Union of Tao and Man is not a rigid or stiff religion. It is a teacher/student system in which each one of us is a teacher and also a student probing our way of life. It is an educational system. We are truly working and serving other people in their lives. Every day we grow and learn. Every day we face the reality of life and see what positive support we can gather from our true life.

We are not idealistic, nor have we formalized a uniform doctrine that says we have to do this or that. There are principles which are time-tested through many generations. You have a right to wonder if those principles can be applied to our time and our life circumstances. If they can, then we feel happy about it and do not have to find a new answer. If they cannot be applied, then what is the reason? Any new answer that can be found to solve the dilemmas and problems of our lives is a contribution to our development and we will be happy about it. Our ancestors in Tao, our forerunners, will not feel bad about new answers, because they enjoy our solutions that are better than theirs. This special feature of Taoist teaching is different from other teachings, where no student can be higher than the teacher. Needing to keep yourself lower than the teacher restrains your growth.

In some ways, every person is a teacher. Also, every person relies on others for something; each can do something better than another. If we were to compete in singing American folk songs, you would do better because I do not know any of them. But if we sing Chinese opera, I would do better because you do not understand it at all. With this example, I think you can feel relaxed. Do not be scared by this older man sitting here. There is no need for that! You are welcome to help me do the work I am doing.

In conventional society - and please be aware that I did not say natural society, but conventional society - people think that men are more helpful to the world in a practical way. That is a limited way of looking at things. Women are also helpful. Women can also be leaders. Whether one is a man or woman, serving the world is not equivalent to being highly visible or being a leader. Some people think that the only serviceable people in society are people with a high education such as psychologists or doctors. Some people measure a person's degree of giving service by money, being very rich like a wealthy doctor or very poor like a Christian saint. Spiritually, the high quality of giving service is much simpler than that. Serving the world is a reality which has no special need for recognition or appreciation from anyone. It comes from your own deep moral nature. If you can truly understand this, then you know that women everywhere, whether in a high or a low position, have made a great contribution to the improvement of worldly life through the generations. They bring about a good life by ameliorating the bad life. A supportive worker is invaluable whether male or female. Some female workers have special personality traits that even make them more helpful and effective than men in certain circumstances.

The point I would like you to understand is that whether a man or woman, what matters most in your life, from a spiritual aspect, is that you give your best effort in whatever situation you find yourself and to whatever you do in life.

So if you have any questions, I would like you to bring them forward so I can answer them for you. All questions are important. A transcription of this discussion will help people who do not have a chance to meet me or bring a question to me, so in that way, you help me do a service. Please do not feel any restraint. Whatever question you have, I am willing to answer.

Q: We have been talking about women's role at the Center and in society. We are a small group of women here at the Center; the men are usually a larger group. What could our role be? What is our role here and in society?

Master Ni: Once we join in studying, there is no difference to be made between men and women. We all need to learn and grow. You might say to yourselves, we are growing with the men so that they can understand us better.

The world is composed of men and women. If you shun opportunities to be close to men, then you will never understand them and they will never understand you. More important than understanding men, however, is first to understand yourself. You can sometimes learn more about yourself by being around men, because sometimes their speech and actions will reflect how you carry yourself or what you believe about yourself. A woman who can learn to carry herself well and has self-respect will never be the one to complain about abuse from men.

Once you understand yourself - I mean in many aspects of yourself, such as your physical strengths and weaknesses, your emotional patterns, skills and talents, etc. - then you can gain an understanding of what direction to take in life. But once you understand yourself energetically - I mean how you use your personal energy - then you will understand men better, because spiritually there is not such a great difference between men and women as there is physically. Personal energy is used through thinking, solving problems, doing physical work, undergoing emotional feelings and expressions, sexual feelings and expressions, expanding out into the world and contracting back into the safety of the home. When you understand how your energy moves and know your energy strengths and shortcomings, you will better be able to understand men's shortcomings and learn how to be around men in a way that is more skillful, more mature and less accusatory.

What shortcomings do modern women have, or women in general? If you investigate the problem on a small, individual scale of your personal self, then you will also have a better understanding about the problems of general society. The only pertinent question is, as an individual, do you learn well, achieve well and allow the worldly masculine energy to assist you? The real issue is not women's liberation or men's liberation or world liberation, it is self-liberation.

When I was a child in elementary school, the girls did better in their lessons. They also did much better in managing personal behavior; I had not even learned to manage myself. I do not have a way to say that women are not smarter than men.

In my country, we men were taught to yield to women. In any circumstance, men were not supposed to compete with women. If they did, people did not sympathize with them. Eventually such a man would be looked down upon by other men and women.

Here in the United States, however, I have a different impression. It often seems like men here are no longer open to giving women a break nor do they try to understand women. American society has been trying to establish a concept of equality between the sexes, even to the point of saying there are no differences between men and women. Some people think that such a concept does not exist, and other people think that this concept has been overemphasized.

Many men see women as being competitive with them in the world. Others do not. In this aspect, I am talking about the business world or the ability to accomplish tasks. Some men recognize that the life of women has a different texture than theirs and give them a break in the requirements of work. Others do not. Regardless of sex, a person can only become a hard-working person through doing lots of work.

Now let us switch to the topic of sexuality. In this new situation where the traditional roles of men as breadwinner and women as housewives have been questioned, sexual roles and the tradition of marriage are less stable. Some men have learned to take everything that is offered by women with no discrimination. By this I mean that many men are in relationships where they obtain help and sexual attention from women without giving anything back. In other words, they do not respond in the traditional way of supporting a woman's life through financial and material compensation and security in return for the gift of her affection and energy.

Some men take women too easily and see them only in brief encounters for sexual purpose. This is partly because these women do not know how to respect and handle themselves. Sexually, women need to learn to give their attention only to the right men, in terms of sexual relationship, and others, in terms of employment and friendship who can value and respect them.

Quite often women act out of emotional need. Perhaps some women do not know how else to act, and because of the cultural promotion and influence, women have many emotional needs. Personal emotion itself creates an entrapment, precipitating a bad situation.

Traditionally, women in general lived a much quieter life. They understood men and could manage them better than today. No man could have taken advantage of a woman; a woman could always manage the situation. Good spiritual work can move in this direction.

My personal experience in school is that boys are usually rough. If we compete with girls intellectually, we are the losers but we discover we can win in sports. So in intellectual achievement under a co-educational system, if the girls give the boys a break, we can usually accomplish as much or more than they can. We need to learn to be the same as women - learn how to be quiet and concentrated - not wild, not grabbing out and becoming scattered, not roaming around.

Young girls in China are usually trained in the advantage of being quiet and concentrated. In modern society, women who are abused become quiet. With spiritual development, those quiet women could prevent a recurrence. That quietude would become a kind of spiritual alertness. If that quality of spiritual alertness would be seen universally among women, I do not think that any man could take advantage of them. Men do not often manifest the quality of intelligence, quiet concentration and self-containment that can be found in a woman.

The problem that creates so much conflict between men and women in their personal relationships and even in the business world is that nowadays, women compete with men, physically and emotionally, instead of quietly and calmly utilizing their intelligence. You might agree that men, because they are physically stronger, have the power to take advantage of women. This occurs a lot in this society, and that is why women are struggling so for what they call equality. However, a wise woman, when she finds a good man, does not use her muscles to compete with him or in fighting to keep him from taking advantage of her. Instead, she uses her intelligence to create a giving relationship in which she cooperates with him and, in return, he offers her protection. Both give, thus nobody takes advantage of anybody else. It is a mutual sharing and equal energy exchange. However, sometimes the woman has to skillfully guide the man to understand his part.

When I was young, many boys had the ambition to have more than one wife because women were such good individuals; they are teachers and models of our deeper spiritual nature. The desire to have many wives is a sort of polytheism among men, because a natural woman is a goddess possessing all the good spiritual qualities, and she enjoys the non-competitive life. To some of you, this sounds ideal but unreal.

In making friends, men usually seek good women. Women sometimes can stay in one position and look over whoever comes along. There is no set pattern about whether the man or the woman is the "hunter." If each is looking, both must respond to the other or no connection is made. Both men and women can make a good choice if they take their time and are wise. From that position of knowing that they have time to choose, they can objectively understand what kind of a person they need to select, or not respond at all.

When it comes time to respond to a man's approach, it never pays for a woman to give herself totally to a man at the beginning. She needs to understand the situation surrounding the man's life and to understand the man. She does not have to be too fastidious or meticulous about her partner. If she is cautious, self-contained, and respectful, she can influence the man to be somewhat less impulsive.

For example, if at the first meeting, for one moment you become loose, the man immediately becomes loose too and does everything. That one second when you give up everything causes him to lose interest totally. "What's your name again?" It is helpful for you to remember that on a date, you are the hostess of a spiritual party. You need to make the spiritual party go well by helping to keep the guest from accidently making a wrong move. Learn to manage it subtly and to conduct it to be enjoyable and productive learning. If you can learn to guide him in a way that does not offend his feelings, then nothing goes wrong.

Do not be carried away by a man's desire. This kind of learning how subtly to manage a situation and a man is a way to attain maturation. This is a secret place from which to attain your growth. It is a great opportunity.

Q: What is your vision of the Centers, here and abroad?

Master Ni: They are self-help schools in which, although I provide the materials, each student can develop a new life of fullness. The students who come to a Center learn to help each other. To me, each individual is a spiritual center. When all the centers come together to establish a bigger Center it becomes a garden of productivity. It means that the individual seeds are sprouting in a better environment to grow into a tree.

I would like each one of you to be a healthy tree and give the fruit to yourself and to the world. In this way you attain your personal growth. Otherwise there is no hope for the world - I say this again. The problems of individuals, societies and the world are consequences of individual spiritual undevelopment.

Look at the condition of the world's religions today; they are self-cheating. People go to them to fool themselves. Liturgical hypnosis does not reach the truth. Religion should be based on improving people's spiritual reality, not on psychological techniques. Psychological skill does not bring people the whole way to maturity and achievement, although it helps on the emotional level and can solve some problems. It is the spiritual truth that helps people find their own centers of being and develop from them.

In religion, people will find only satisfaction, consolation or emotional gratification, which is not the healthy way. Surely, people need consolation and correct support for their spiritual attainment. People need warmth from truly healthy friendships. Those things can come from our own growth; if they do not come from our growth, they are false and shallow. For example, if a child is paid ten dollars to run an errand for an adult, the child is happy. But if the child uses the ten dollars to go to the ice cream shop and buys two quarts of ice cream and eats all of it, believe me, this is ruin. A spiritual center is not an ice cream store; it will not sell you something that tastes good but undermines your health. It is a garden that you cultivate with your friends. It is a place to realize a Heavenly paradise on earth. It is possible.

Q: What made you decide to come to the United States and bring your tradition to us?

Master Ni: America is young and hopeful. I have made many friends here because the people are open to the teachings. American friends have a lot of strength and openness and so are able to bring about a new way of life. Truth itself is a power. Conventional teaching blocks the mind and the eyes, so people who are in an open society like America and who are looking for deeper truth need the opportunity brought by this Tradition.

American women are different from women in other parts of the world with conventional knowledge. They have the spirit of independence and freedom. It would be great if they would devote themselves to looking for true spiritual growth. You need to apply freedom toward the right goal.

When I was in Taiwan, as an established teacher and doctor of traditional Chinese medicine, many American students and patients came to me. One day, they extended an invitation to me to come over here. I accepted because I thought that this is where I would like to be. It is a country that is open enough to look for the truth.

In the beginning, during the first year, the people who came to me were people who experienced disappointment in this culture. They thought that I could offer them an evasive path. Some of them learned about oriental religions and concluded that spirituality means that you do not need to work and you do not need to achieve anything. They believed that God provides everything and we just need to know how to enjoy it. And they believed that if you do not enjoy it enough, you can always use drugs. I have corrected those students. I directed them into a correct life, doing good work.

If I can see the essence in an individual, I value it and help to develop it. At times I was not happy because it seemed as though there was no true understanding of my teaching. Then, after that initial experience, my true work began. The true purpose of my being here is to teach and to write.

Q: So you thought the time was right, that we in the United States would be able to understand and appreciate what you had to offer?

Master Ni: Yes. Students can make use of my teaching if they are sincere. Spiritual learning needs concentration or it will not serve you correctly. When I was in many places like this, I saw intelligent women students doing as well as men students in the material sphere of life. One or two, however, turned the learning opportunity for spiritual growth into a social opportunity instead. Unfortunately, they were not really open to the study of the material and of the teaching I gave. They did not attain their growth. You know, one way to learn is to take the rocky way of learning the long, hard lessons about life and social opportunity. Some people never learn anything that way but just get lost. However, it is possible to avoid trouble through dedicated study and self-help. An aware person can do very well.

The Center can be a place to learn together with spiritual friends and find mutual support instead of a hunting ground for a husband or wife, boyfriend or girlfriend. Hold the attitude, "I will make this Center a place of healthy growth. I do not expect anything negative to happen to me or because of me." Then, by holding that attitude and by concentrating on your learning, you help each other grow; then we can enjoy genuine friendship. A true spiritual friendship is better than any other relationship; it can be much closer than a brother, sister, father or mother. A family or relatives can come together to join in the learning at one of the Centers, too. Any such spiritual relationship is a Heavenly relationship and certainly better than one of merely worldly intent.

I cannot be here with you physically all the time, so I am happy the study group system is working to facilitate your helping one another. The study group is basically for you. Let me give you a rule of thumb: If there is a teaching given, look for its usefulness and make it connect with the learning of the group. This is a way to help one another in realizing what you learned intellectually.

I heard that you have studied a chapter in the *Gentle Path of Spiritual Progress* where it refers to a book called *The Red Chamber* and that it upset some of you. Perhaps you still do not understand it or see the point. In any case, one discussion about something does not necessarily complete the job. Any one talk may not complete the work to be done because all events can be seen from many ways of understanding. You can ask me again about that chapter and we will find the right answer. Sometimes a person needs to stand back and view things from a different angle to see the point.

Q: I think what was bothersome was that the teaching said a woman should be subservient and stand behind a man.

Master Ni: Subservience was an old-fashioned way of saying "selfless service," and standing behind someone is called helpful support. In a spiritual relationship, each person makes a gift of service and support to the other person. In a relationship, service and support are important; they becomes especially important on a large view.

If a man has a certain position in society and accomplishes a large task, we say that "Behind every great man is a great woman." I say that behind a great man there are many great women and many great men, and vice versa. No one single person can accomplish a significant task, no matter whether that person is a man or a woman. If any one woman accomplishes a great work, behind this woman there must be many great women and great men who have given their assistance.

Usually the relationship between a man and woman is quite sensitive. In this, it is like your eye; a tiny piece of sand immediately makes you uncomfortable. You cannot stand it. Similarly, a relationship has to be pure, kept clean and misunderstandings need to be cleared up. If it is fitting, the woman can work behind the scenes to let the man accomplish the big thing out front. This also means, if the woman is a great leader and has leader energy, that the man can be behind the scenes and help her to accomplish her goal. It is not a fact that being out in front is better or being behind the scenes is better. That is not the question. Sometimes it is a challenge if you continue seeing only the surface. Your maturity or growth can help you look at the deeper reality that is beyond the surface level of any situation.

Q: I guess the whole thing is that something important is being done, and whoever can carry it out in the front does that part.

Master Ni: Right. In spiritual learning, the focus is to get the job done, and it does not matter so much what role each one has. There must be cooperation between the person at the front and the helper in the rear. I know that some American women like to compete with men and some men like to compete with women. In general, the competition is for salaries to support children. This is very necessary in our culture. But no matter who is in front or on top, everybody on a team is important. It takes everybody to accomplish any large thing.

And about enjoyment, the workers in front do not necessarily enjoy themselves more than those behind the scenes. In old China, the women were usually wiser than the men; they made the men work hard while they managed the routine of life. They all enjoyed themselves. Do you believe it or not?

Q: I've been brought up that women have to be kind, loving and accepting. At times I find myself not really being
able to see other people as they are, but I just go ahead
and be nice. Then I feel like my feelings have been
stomped on, or I have not protected myself, or I have given
my trust or something else away to a person. I feel violat-
ed in the sense that I am not able to tell what that person
is like. I would like to better develop my intuition and my
discernment of people.

Master Ni: Many women, because of the conditioning you
mentioned, have trouble with two things. One is learning
to say no. Women are too afraid of negative repercus-
sions, which in most situations in modern life might be
minimal or nonexistent; sometimes a small instant nega-   ⁓
tive prevents a big future negativity. In other situations,
they have reasons for this fear. Thus, the second thing is
learning to avoid those situations which bring about con-
frontations in the first place.

　　As I see you, first you need to know your position in
different circumstances. For example, different occasions
need different adjustments. When you work, you need to
be straight in your work. You need to handle people who
try to invade the scope of your responsibility. And never
let anyone utilize a work connection to manipulate you in
a personal way. Working relationships are totally different
from social or personal relationships.

　　If you have desire or a wish to have a man for company, then open your eyes wide and quietly survey your
opportunities. If at first you can distinguish different
opportunities and make these opportunities serve you,
you are smart. I think you are developed enough to dis-
cern the right person. But do not mix everything up and
confuse yourself. You cannot mix business contacts and
your personal life. Family life is family life. School is
school, work is work, study group is study group. There
is no connection between them and you need to keep
them separate in terms of your attitudes and responses to
them. When a special opportunity or special occasion

arises, apply your knowledge to see if it is a right beginning for you or not.

Let's say you see a tall, handsome man who is well-dressed. Even if the situation is right for you, you still need to approach the person carefully, because you do not know the true physical condition of the person. Perhaps the person has herpes or AIDS or some other disease or imbalance. Never give yourself trouble by confusing different kinds of opportunities or channels, saying, any man that comes along is a man. No. Each one is a different kind of personality!

Do not be crazy about men. If you are psychologically and emotionally dependent and you maintain the longing for a man, then you yourself create an opportunity for your downfall. It is like a self-ambush, a self-programmed interruption of your positive achievements. If you do not wish this to happen, you must take steps to improve your emotional condition.

Q: I'm not quite clear about that.

Master Ni: If you have a yearning for a man, it can become the foundation of a trap, a self-programmed trap that invites trouble. This yearning can be something as simple as a feeling of loneliness and a desire for companionship, not just a sexual desire. Then when the first man comes along, your desires and longings are so strong that you do not access your self-control, strength and objectivity to avoid a potentially unhelpful situation.

If you have attained spiritual and emotional independence, you do not need to rely on a man for companionship or support. This means that if a man is there, you are strong. If there is no man there for you, you are still strong. If a good opportunity comes along, you still have the reservoir of strength to check it out very carefully before you decide what to do.

Q: If a person develops herself independently as you said, and then an opportunity comes along . . .

Master Ni: Let us take an example. I am sitting here, and you are sitting at my side. It is a chance for me to make your acquaintance. Then, in finding out about you, I understand your situation and focus on how I can help you. This is an example of clearly directing my thoughts and energy in one direction and not mixing anything up.

If, instead, I sit here as your spiritual teacher I think, "I'm going to make this woman go to bed with me," it becomes a totally different situation. You have come to learn from me; if I try to make it anything different from a teacher-student relationship, I will confuse you and you will never learn from me. Instead, I would poison you. Not only that, but the energy confusion would cause me to lose your trust as a student.

Conversely, if you have the intent of pursuing me sexually or for companionship, then that also interrupts the chance of an educational type of exchange. Such a motivation would interfere with the energy exchange of teaching and learning.

Let us say that I am not a man of spiritual discipline, just another ordinary Chinese fellow. I'm available, healthy and handsome. I still need to find out if the woman I am interested in has a boyfriend. If she does, I had better not pursue her; why cause trouble? On the other hand, if a woman is interested in a fellow who is pursuing her, she also needs to find out the similar details before she gets involved. At least have as much of knowledge as possible.

So all the time you need to put your antennae out. The whole idea is, learn to be independent and stand on your own. Then, if an appropriate opportunity presents itself, you can join in a relationship, but still maintain a sense of your own independence. A woman really needs to be clear about her goals first; then when her mind is clear, she can put her antennae out to look for the appropriate match.

Q: It seems like it would be hard for a woman to maintain her independence and for a man to maintain his while at the same time trying to merge together and work towards a union or marriage.

Master Ni: Actually, it is much better, much happier. Independence is a state of mind. It does not mean that the two people live apart and do not relate. Ideally, each person keeps his or her own state of mind while giving support to the other. That is different from emotional reliance, or trying to take something from the other person. Emotional reliance is not trustworthy because a relationship might break up, the man might change or the woman might change. Then, in one fast shift, either the man or the woman - or both - suffers a lot.

For example, now you love your boyfriend very much. Let us say that it is 100% devotion, pure love. If he loses interest and changes, then how will you handle yourself? Some people become crazy and the situation is terrible. Instead of engaging in craziness, try holding this attitude: "I love you but also I respect myself. I also trust myself. If today you leave me because I have done something wrong or something else has pulled you away, it is agreeable. You go ahead." In this position, with this attitude, you will not suffer by his leaving you or by your losing him. This is not an attitude of not caring, because of course you care. It is an attitude of strength, indicating you have the ability to rely on yourself. It makes your relationship a choice, not a desperate need. If you make yourself a valuable partner, the man will not leave.

In such a relationship, you do not program trouble for yourself; you only correct your errors when you make them. You keep your focus on learning, growing, changing yourself, refining and improving yourself to be a better person. If you have that appreciation, you will enjoy him and enjoy his company. The spiritual stability of being centered and flexibly strong is irresistible to other people; they will seek you out instead of trying to avoid or escape you.

Self-reliance means that no occasion arises where you conclude that he has something wrong with him and you have something wrong with yourself. Viewing things with self-reliance, you will keep from self-complaining, self-pity and self-disappointment. The old way, of being desperate or needy, is nonsense. It is also self-damaging.

So first, stand on your steady feet in any circumstance. This is easy to say but not do without help unless you practice it by trying it yourself. This type of spiritual learning can become part of your personality. Whether you are old or young does not matter. Nobody, man or woman, wants to choose a partner who will become like a weight tied around one's neck.

For example, let us say that your husband comes home from work one day with a long, horse face. You are bothered and wonder if you have done something wrong and if he does not love you any more. You might just remain quiet for a while. After he has finished processing and understanding his trouble, he may come and tell you about it. First, self-confidence: "I did nothing wrong." Then understanding: "Oh, he had trouble with his business, he had trouble with his students." If you can help, help. If you cannot help, it is not your responsibility. You do not need to be overly sensitive or anxious.

Remember, when you see your man coming home with a horse face, do not be bothered. If you keep yourself calm, he immediately notices it and says to himself, "How can I bring trouble and anger back to my woman? It is unreasonable." Let him have a chance to see his own emotion and to correct himself. Then there will be union and happiness. Do not push things. If you push him to talk about it, it is usually not as relaxed as if he comes around by himself to tell you about it. This is the ideal, of course.

Q: I think I can do that now, but it took me a long time to get to that point. Does that have anything to do with non-attachment?

Master Ni: If you are not in some way attached to the other person, it is not deep love. But even with your attachment and caring, you still realize that each moment is a new moment. There is no protection for anything in the world. Your only protection is the new moment. Each new moment you handle yourself correctly, express yourself correctly and enjoy your partner correctly is true love and true life. If the reality of the energy between you has changed and you keep thinking it still exists the old way, then you are living in your imagination, not in the reality of the moment. It is to think, "We are already fixed, already married and this is the custom."

To some women, love and an old-fashioned type of marriage are everything. But a woman might consider, "I am also an individual in the world, so besides marriage, I need intellectual development, social development and my own spiritual development, etc. I am not an ox or a donkey, tied by a rope to a stick." If a woman balances herself, she will not concentrate or demand too much from one man.

Let us say that a man and woman married when they were young. After five or ten years, the man or woman does not love the other one any more. Why? If the man works in the world every day, he may grow a lot; but has the woman grown emotionally, intellectually, in worldly knowledge and living skills, in learning to make a happier relationship? Or is she still the same person she was when they met, still like a 17-year old girl? It is natural and it happens sometimes. If there is a growth difference between the partners, the marriage will fall apart. So a marriage must allow for the growth of each individual. In most cases, this means that the husband must have the courage to let the wife develop her interests, but the wife then needs to do it in a way that brings energy back to the relationship.

Or let us say that it is the woman who has had a lot of growth. The man sees that the woman has changed and that the relationship is not sweet any more. Then he feels self-pity. He feels inferior. He feels inadequate in the match and his happiness goes away. In this case, the woman needs to curb any desire she has for a more interesting man and find a positive way to help the husband make himself become more interesting to her.

If you lose the husband because of not enough growth, you can still learn to be a desirable woman for any smart, appreciative man. If the fault is on the man's side, it is not helpful for you to be sad over this development, because it is his situation. You cannot force your self to be accepted.

Be aware also of another thing that is more profound, which is that all people have cycles called human destiny. Some men and women are suitable for marriage but some are not. Some women can marry husbands who are supportive and sweet and others marry men who are rough, cruel and selfish. Either way, it is destiny. If your destiny is not suitable for being with a man, no matter what effort you make, it is not possible to have a man at your side.

Thus, if a man comes into your life who is sweet, nice and supportive, then this is your destiny. Destiny is why there are so many undeserving women who marry handsome, supportive husbands. Also, there are many intelligent, beautiful women who cannot get a husband. If they were to talk to "God," they might say: "You are unfair, you treat me so badly." However, fate and destiny are still external experience. We need to check out our internal reality to bear the real flower and fruit in our lives.

For example, if you see an unattractive or unskilled woman who has caught the love and attention of a good man, you may wonder what the attraction is. Usually she has a special virtue or special advantage that cannot be seen with the eyes. If you develop yourself enough, you will understand this better.

Yesterday, I was in another Center helping some students. One woman I was with was young and beautiful and had lots of artistic talent. She had different experiences with men, but her relationships always ended up in unhappiness. Another woman, who is older and divorced with two children, married a man who is older than she is and supportive. He was glad to take care of her and the two boys. The younger woman, who was more intelligent and in a stronger position in society, did not see the good, positive virtues in the other woman. I

pointed it out. I think the message came through and
that she understood.

If a woman is too assertive and strong, a man will
usually treat her like another man. If you are a traditional, conventional lady type - by this I mean, dignified, gentle and respectable - you can find a man who is protective
and supportive.

So notice how you organize and project your own
energy. Fortune or destiny is decided by your internal
energy, more than how you make up your mind. By that I
mean, if you are strong and gentle inside, you will find
strength and gentleness outside. If you are sloppy and
rough inside, you will see the same reflected outside,
reflected in yourself and sometimes in the man you find.
Once you see clearly, you will know how to arrange yourself in a way that will suit you better. Sometimes you
need to discipline yourself to get what you wish to have.
If you find you are one way and wish to change, I suggest
that you read the sections on sincerity and balance in my
other books.

*Q: If a woman is in a relationship, supporting and serving
the man as you were talking about before, is it still important that she not forget about her own life?*

Master Ni: What is your own life?   It is not your social
life.   It is not your business life.   It is your body, mind and
spirit.   You know, a woman can support a man and have
a wonderful time and have a wonderful life.   It depends on
the woman, her attitudes, her development and the kind
of man she finds.

This is what I was talking about to my friend yesterday.   The way you keep a man is to serve the man.   Make
the man feel like a man, then he will not go away from
you.   But you still need to know if the man is worth it or
not.   Many men are not worth it.   Why does a woman
bother to take care of a man like that?   He is like a tree
that never gives any fruit.   Do not waste your time.

You need to examine your concept of what life is.   Life
is not only the modern concept of having a work life, a

social life, 2.5 children, and owning a house and car. It is not being a stereotyped definition of anything. That is still external. True spiritual life depends on your inner being. Anything that comes from inside out that is truthful and sincere is the hallmark of real life.

All of you are working in the world. Before, women generally worked inside the home and men worked outside. Either way, all have to work. They used to say women were dependent upon their husbands because women were financially dependent. But now, everybody earns money. It was mentioned to me that because American women have become so strong, the men have become weak. Some of them cannot work and not only that, some of them cannot cook or do anything. A useful man will never allow himself to become like that. His reality of living makes that far from his everyday truth.

Before, in ancient times, men worked in the fields and women worked inside, maintaining a harmonious family life. Women who stayed inside to take care of the babies also had chickens and hogs to feed and other hard work to do. You cannot say that women depended on men; eventually the men came home and needed warm food to eat. They helped each other.

Today, some inferior men become dependent on women. They take advantage; they say, "I'm going to live with you, stay with you." But once they move in, they do not do anything. They say, "Feed me." Because the woman believes she needs a man, she does everything to take care of him. It is not fruitful. It is a poison. What does the man do? Just plays turtle. Such a man is not worth much because he has no sense and no creative energy.

Q: That is the way it seems to be in today's society, that women not only keep up the home but they provide for themselves. So a lot of men think, "Because she provides for herself emotionally and financially, what do I need to do for her? There is nothing I need to do for her."

Master Ni: A good man still says, if my wife works, I can contribute my energy to produce more happiness. If I make more, we can have time to take a vacation. We can enjoy our old age, we can give a good education to our kids. It depends on whom you marry. Relationship does not have to be based upon need; it can also be based upon giving.

Also, you can delegate responsibilities so that each of you cares for different departments of life and yet are mutually caring for each other.

Q: Is it disadvantageous to be a woman? Is it considered inferior to be born a woman?

Master Ni: No. To be either a man or a woman is to have both advantages and disadvantages.

On one level, usually people are impressed that women are more sexy than men and that the problem of sexual pressure in women is stronger than in men. That is true of certain people with certain lifestyles. For example, men do not notice their internal sexual pressure when they engage in sports, go to war, fight, or hunt. Those things, sports and war, are not necessary to life; they are mostly an expression, transformation or transfer of sexual pressure into outward activities. In general, if women mostly stay at home and do not do things as vigorously as men do, they will experience stronger sexual pressure than men.

However, I am not encouraging women to do the same activities as men to reduce their internal sexual pressure. I am saying, as I have on many occasions, that if a man or woman cannot easily fulfill their sexual need, it is better to find a way to transfer that energy into spiritual energy. Even if a spiritual person lives a general life with the correct partner, the sexual aspect can be properly fulfilled. It does not mean that a spiritual person absolutely cannot have sex. That is not the way. If that were the way, a person would be overextended spiritually and neglect his or her own physical condition. If young or middle aged, this can cause a lot of trouble, because there will be a physical compensation in dreams or in other physical manifestations.

Q: Do you mean energy needs its expression, either sexually or in other ways?

Master Ni: If you wish to live a normal life, that is good guidance. However, some people also have spiritual ambition. They wish to attain spiritual immortality, to live after death. Or they have a particular spiritual purpose or learning and need concentration. Generally, if you have a spiritual goal, you can find correct sexual fulfillment with the right partner.

Sexual practice depends on response. The person at your side is not you. He or she is a different person, with different psychological and physical cycles. You cannot force another person into sex; that would not be beneficial. Sex needs natural attraction and natural response. That fulfillment is usually less harmful; at least it is a healthy way of fulfillment.

In ancient times, wise people knew that sexual energy was their physical foundation and could form people's lives differently. They did not allow themselves to contact or see anything to tempt them into sexual activity or make them desirous, because they wanted to maintain themselves in a natural condition. Generally speaking, we do not need to be too sexual; that can be artificial. The right amount of sex for an individual does not come from any imaginary or psychological pressure, but from a response to physical need. Usually imaginary or psychological pressures cause people to have sex more often than is needed. In modern times, human culture is confused. It is so complicated now that people lose the naturalness and normalcy of the human sexual sphere.

For example, let us talk about the grizzly bear. Only once a year when the female is ovulating does she become receptive. Otherwise, she just walks away. This is normal. Bears do not have sexy magazines or advertisements to arouse them at unnatural times.

Modern people, if they are married, have an obligation to do whatever the wife or husband needs or does not need. The wife needs to do it with her husband. Yet, the correct focus is to do it in a way healthy for both.

General adult life is complicated. People act mostly out of psychological needs promoted by commercial advertisements and so forth. This is the lower level of culture. Their sexual knowledge is even worse than that of a mother bear. When a person's energy is full in that department, you can do it and enjoy; that is a healthy way to fulfill it. But if the energy is not there, and only a person's mind is there, when he or she does it, the woman does not become wet and it is done artificially. That causes damage to a woman's organs and brings cancer and so forth. Modern women's knowledge of sexual hygiene is sometimes poorer than that of the bear! So in that way, they cannot be proud. They do not really have any knowledge about themselves. Or they are pressured by their partners at a time when they are not in a good cycle.

So what am I recommending for women? This answer will not entirely come from me, but it will come from your own growth and understanding. Some principles of sexual health and hygiene are recommended, but mostly in real practice, you still need to know yourself. The body is your own machine. You are the one that operates it and uses it. You can damage it or you can make it continue to serve you.

In this conversation, I am not involved in saying how to transfer a woman's sexual energy into spiritual energy. Some time later I will give you the esoteric teaching of a woman's cultivation. But there is one thing all of you can learn from this small talk: the healthy performance of sex. Do not be motivated by pornography or the culture of general society. Do not be motivated by stimulating food or by watching anything else which can make you feel sexy, because that is artificial and not true. If anything you do is artificial and not true, it is damaging. The minimum recommendation I would like to make here is, after you become an adult, think about how much sex you have out of real need and how much out of psychological fantasy.

Q: What can a married woman or a woman dependent on a man do if the man pressures her too much or her energy is not there?

Master Ni: In one type of good relationship, the man works outside the house. The woman stays home and she is prepared for the man. When the man comes home and has some need, the woman cooperates. That is called harmony. If her energy is not there, she makes him some healthy and tasty food, tells a story for him so he can enjoy a good laugh, they watch a movie on television together or she does something else for him. She just makes him calm so that he knows that she loves him, and that this time they need to do something else. That is better than playing the game of two kinds of muscles.

Unfortunately, poor people do not have much fun. They go to bed early, so they create many children. Rich people have too much wine, so they cannot have good descendants because wine damages the seeds and eggs. So as a spiritual teacher, I would like people to awaken and look for the natural practice in their lives.

A good marriage is wonderful. A bad marriage is a kind of unnatural, false imposing relationship with no benefit. It is harmful. So there does not need to be any rigid law about divorce or no divorce, whether a person can marry only one partner for the whole life or have many partners. The question is on an energy level: what can you handle that will bring the high quality and happiness that you are truly looking for? What is one person's poison is somebody else's meat. It is enriching to understand yourself on that level. What I am talking about here is not achieving yourself on a high level nor the goal of life. I am talking about how you handle your machine, the body; that is important. Few people know how to use their bodies well.

Specialized cultivations are given only to women who have really decided to do spiritual cultivation. This means they do not need sexual fulfillment anymore. If my students only do half of spiritual learning, I can only give half. We do not like to suggest that all people be celibate.

Celibacy is only for people who, in their destiny and self-recognition, find that a different way would be more enjoyable. This way makes them happier than only living to please a woman or a man. That is a different process.

The teaching of my tradition cannot be assertive. We know that each individual is born with different energy. This is especially pronounced when a person grows into a family and a society, which all of us do. Usually a young person's sexual psychology is already formed by the family. As an individual, if you think you are acting on an unnatural tendency learned from your family or society, you can work on it yourself to correct it. Those things damage your joy of life. That includes general religion, too.

Q: When I read the story of Quan Yin in The Gentle Path of Spiritual Progress, it really spoke to me. I have been wondering in the past few months exactly what is a woman's relationship to Quan Yin and how can a woman deepen that relationship.

Master Ni: Quan Yin is a model of graceful spiritual energy. Anyone who achieves herself or himself is a Quan Yin, at least to have the wisdom that helps a woman rise above emotional suffering. To rise above one's own suffering is more of a spiritual achievement and personal energy sublimation than being a person of such and such worldly attainment or position.

Just like Quan Yin, many Taoist women achieved themselves with a special practice that teaches sublimation of spiritual energy. There is both sexual energy sublimation into spiritual energy and spiritual energy sublimation into the achieved soul. Spiritual energy can be converged and is transformable. When spiritual energy remains in its natural purity and gentleness, the name of Jade Maiden is given to it. It is beyond gender.

However, the image of Quan Yin, or other images, have been promoted by general religion as external worship instead of internal cultivation. I would like to point this out for your own cultivation. Quan Yin is a pure projection of the high spiritual energy of a woman herself or of a man himself. Using the image or figure of the Quan Yin is just a method for cultivating your own spiritual energy; she is an image of your own soul.

If you take up spiritual cultivation, use Quan Yin as an example, a mental image. Say, "This kind of pure energy, white energy, this shape made of light: I would like to be this kind of a spiritual being." Set up your shrine like that.

I will teach you some invocations separately that communicate particularly with Quan Yin. When you do them, it produces spiritual joy and power similar to spiritual independence. Internal sufficiency is a spiritual power; it is a much greater power than relating with someone.

Some women suffer in the ocean of life; sometimes they enjoy relationships with males and sometimes they do not. Sometimes a relationship finally becomes a broken bubble, with nothing left. If you are wise enough, you can decide whether your own personal life path or personal fortune is suitable for male companionship. If a woman has a lot of money, she could keep a lot of men at her house and make them serve her, but I do not know if she will be happy.

Once in China there was a woman emperor. She had a group of men concubines. When she was in her eighties, she still enjoyed sex. In written history, it has been recorded that only one or two women did that. Generally speaking, I do not suggest that anyone keep many concubines. If you like, you can do it, if you have that kind of energy to waste.

This group of women here today is special. In Los Angeles, for example, there are many different small newspapers that one can find in newsstands, where a woman will describe herself, put in her picture, and write what size breasts she has, what kind of man she needs, and what size male reproductive organ she needs. The men put their picture in the newspaper too. I am not kidding; it is a real thing. At the beginning I was startled to find out about such things. Later, I found out that America is a free society and this is a part of the freedom.

It is freedom, but not a good education. It represents no spiritual growth. I prefer that none of you abuse your life like that. I would rather that all of you learn from Quan Yin to maintain your good energy to achieve high spiritual beingness, and not pull yourselves down for just a little sexual fun that carries with it a lot of pain and suffering.

We are a small minority. I do not mind that we are a minority. And I am not afraid of people saying to me, Master Ni, your teaching is as rigid as the Christian teaching. In truth, my spiritual advice to you is different. You are not a nun. You choose to support yourself, and you do not live on other people's donations. You can project Quan Yin's energy, not only in your spiritual practice, but in your life, too.

In this moment you can be a Quan Yin, too; why? Because in this moment you have contacted me, as I observe, you have been wise enough to make me talk to you and conduct myself in a gracious way of giving advice. It can be a similar situation in the study group: you can make all the men become wise, because you respect yourselves highly. When you sit quietly, your spiritual energy subtly influences and affects people and brings out their positive side, too. That is the goodness you can attain.

If you are looking for another man, and if it is the same old story, what is fun about it? Are you crazy? In this moment, wake up. It is the right moment to wake up. In learning about men, some women think they had bad experiences in the past. However, the past experience is not a bad experience; it is a creative experience because now you have awakened yourself by learning from it. The past experience is poison if you are still longing for relationship, marriage or men to keep at your side with your old attitudes.

I believe you have already seen the fruits and poisons of sexual relationship. I think you understand what is real growth and real happiness. Women have sexual fluid, sexual energy; moved downward, it becomes children. Moved upwards, it makes women become angels. What is your choice? It is all decided by you.

My teaching has different levels. On one level, I promote balanced, decent, healthy practice, even sexuality. I do not want to make all women and men celibate. But on a high level, a woman will decide when she has had enough. It comes, not out of sadness, but out of growth. Then I consider her my true friend. I can help her more. She is one step closer to our spiritual goal.

Sexual interest is natural. If people overly focus on it, they worship sex. They work for sex. They live for sex. The suffer for sex. They suffer for it, as brave as the soldiers go to the battlefield. All of the people who stay that way are drowning in the waves of the ocean of life; suffering, drowning and sinking down into the depths. There are people who land on the shore and save their spiritual energy which is the energy when it is applied in that direction. Only being overindulgent in sex harms spiritual health.

If a young person has a good partner, there is a chance to fulfill that part of life in a good way, because spiritual cultivation can also have life companionship. I am not saying that you have to change your whole life situation if you do not have that kind of comfortable company. You do not need to go look for somebody else to make your life be right. You are complete in yourself. You are the mother and you are the father. Your head is the father and your belly is the mother. When you make those two parts, yin and yang energy, have intercourse, you bring about your spiritual baby as described in my books.

It is hard for all of you. You are all still young. Also you have a menstruation cycle that brings the energy down. There is a way to do cultivation to correct and change that physical situation; then you really are achieved.

Q: What is the practice to stop the menstruation cycle?

Master Ni: At your age and stage of life, it is not healthy or beneficial. It is not bringing something to a stop mechanically. It is an energy transformation, taking that cycle to be something else. The body of a healthy young woman produces lots of eggs. But by doing this practice, the eggs are killed, and become useless. Not one survives. So you can see that this is a very serious thing. Before the eggs are even formed, they are already transformed to become life energy.

I learned Taoist training much earlier than my experience of married life. I know that it is of no benefit to be with someone if the partner does not have the same understanding. But where can a person find the right woman or man who is loving and understanding? If you have higher growth, you have more difficulty finding appropriate company. So after the fulfillment of my natural obligation in marriage and childraising, I changed my life. I have also experienced different sexual fulfillment, but gradually I have stopped the ordinary way. Long before I stopped, I had achieved the total transformation of the energy. It is beneficial to my spiritual work; that is why I can be still active and busy in giving service.

So, I have already transformed this energy to be my spiritual work energy. Any person who transfers that energy in this direction can have better health and move toward higher spiritual development.

I am always encouraging all of you to learn and to work. The world needs good teachers and it needs correct guidance. To be achieved women, you not only bring the benefit of wisdom into your own life, but you bring your wise life into the lives of all people. Can you do that? You can. Definitely you can. If you have any hesitation, it is because you still press yourselves down by the old way, not feeling fulfilled in the worldly life. By living the spiritual way, you will make all life experience be your spiritual cultivation.

Q: I do shiatsu massage. I have read that when doing massage on people you can take their sins into yourself. Is that true?

Master Ni: Massage is usually not a good profession for women. Do not let men make you into a sexual object, physically or through their thoughts and emotions.

Q: I do not do men any more, just women. But sometimes very sick women, sick with cancer.

Master Ni: The simple thing to do afterwards is to wash your hands.

Q: I always do that carefully. Several weeks ago I worked with a woman and afterward the entire house seemed as though it were filled with some kind of poison in the atmosphere.

Master Ni: Also, you can go out and "poof" the energy, exhale outside, and put the bad energy into the dirt. By poofing, I mean blow it out through your mouth like blowing out a candle. Then breathe fresh air inside to purify yourself. If it is serious trouble, then purify yourself with sun energy. Solar energy and lunar energy can be used to purify yourself.

Q: You are the living representative of the yang energy.

Master Ni: No, I am Quan Yin inside, which is beyond gender and form. You see, I have already cut off most of my desire and turned my energy inwardly. I have already integrated myself and my own energy to grow my spiritual fruit. An appropriate spiritual goal is to be a being above the discrimination of gender. Though the male energy is still active and alive, that energy is transformed.

Q: Well, your gender subjects you to having more yang energy so your goal is to balance the yin and the yang, whereas we females, have more yin and have to bring up the yang. I do not know who Quan Yin was, so maybe I am being redundant, but who can we model ourselves after? You obviously, as the master.

Master Ni: There is a model. We have a poster of a man, and usually a woman needs a man's energy, so it can help you too. It is a poster of Master Lu, Tung Ping. He achieved himself close to one thousand years ago, I believe. After his ascendence, he still continued his worldly work.

Your question is valuable. You know that because you are a woman, you need a man's energy to support you. It is the universal yang energy. There are two levels of yang energy. One level, as I mentioned, is the spiritual image of the model of Master Lu; on the other level, the universal yang energy is the solar energy. It is representative of manly or masculine energy. The moon usually represents feminine energy.

My achieved students know where their masculine energy comes from. Do you know the secret of the origin of masculine energy? Male energy is from the sun. Men eat beef and fish and make their sexual organ strong, but from where comes the beef and the fish? They all come from the sun. Our life comes from the sun.

You see, seriously speaking, we are born complete. Deeply within our head is the yang, masculine energy. The mind, in the center of the body, is neutral; it has no discrimination of male or female, but the lower part or abdomen is the feminine energy. The secret of a balanced life is supported by internal energy intercourse. If you can make those two energies communicate and exchange, this will bring about the spiritual flower, fruit and seeds. This is how we grow spiritually in order to attain spiritual immortality. It is the most valuable thing to do. I hope that some day all of you can achieve that level.

Q: Master Ni, since a woman's energy is low because of the menstrual cycle, should we carry our energy in the middle tan tien in our daily practice?

Master Ni: Right. Usually you hold it in the point between the nipples. Always maintain the energy in this region and circle it by mental conducting and do not let it sink down. This has two benefits. One benefit is because your energy is full there, then the secretion in the breasts is good and it helps prevent lumps; it has the value of rejuvenation. The second is that you are not wet all the time. Maybe when you are young, if you see an attractive man, you become wet. But when you keep the energy in the point between the nipples and avoid looking for stimulation, you become wise and use energy for enriching your life.

If the energy is in your head, you are nervous and always have tension. But if you calmly keep your energy here in your center, it will come up again easily. Just maintain it there if you do not like to have your energy rushing up or rushing down. It is beneficial.

This is called the middle tan tien. Tan tien means storage room or internal workshop for medicine or immortal power storage and refinement center.

Q: *This is kind of personal, but when I was a little girl, I never got boy crazy like all the other girls. When I was in high school, I never cared to date; I always liked to stay home and read or play with my dog. Later, when I became involved with someone whom I later married, I was partly interested in the fact that someone was interested in me, but I was never crazy about the idea. It was just such an extension of my energy. I guess I got into a marriage because I romantically believed that a woman was not complete if she was not with a man. Back then, we were made to believe that every woman had to be complete in this way.*

Everybody thought it was kind of weird that I was not looking for a man all the time. I have never really been man oriented, even though I would eventually like to have that perfect union. People have always told me I was striving for the ideal. After my divorce, I never went to bars to pick up men, and I have had very limited sexual experience, but I do not feel bad about any of that.

Master Ni: This is uncommon. It is good, and you are using spiritual study to complete your life. I am glad about that. You use all your life changes well.

Yesterday I saw a patient who said she saw a psychologist for many years to clear up that type of suffering. So you are great. I consider you a heroine.

Q: Is that something that society teaches us? On television, they match people up so young.

Master Ni: It is the commercial culture. People are conditioned by advertisements and social fashion. They condition youngsters to start sexual life early. That is not really a beneficial or good thing to do.

Q: By my society's standards, I should have been sent to a psychiatrist, I started so late, sexwise. But I felt that I started too early.

Master Ni: If you can manage it and are not bothered, it would be to your benefit to live alone without a man. But it is good for you to join a group of spiritual friends. Now, you might like men to change their attitude and way of thinking. You do not want them to think, "Here is this mature woman; maybe I can relate to her sexually."

How do you get men to change their attitude towards you? Be spiritually centered. If you change the impression that men and women have of you, then women do not think that you are one of the competition, and men do not think that you can be abused. You can talk gently, be helpful in learning, and never exchange sexual communication by looking at a man or a woman's eye. Some people consider it polite to look people in the eye in conversation, but that is among family members or close friends. Do not look directly in a man's eyes even in business contact, unless you wish to initiate something. Look at a different part of his face or something instead. It is said that the eyes are the windows to the soul. When your gazes meet, it is already a kind of intercourse or energy blending, so know a person well before you look into their eyes. You can talk uprightly or express yourself uprightly without especially expressing something like, "I need your attention." Always remain spiritually centered, then you are a good example for other people.

In general circumstances, for all men or woman, married or unmarried, the mind is crazy. The mind is loose and erotic. Physically maybe a person is not, but the mind is that way. What is the benefit of that? There is no benefit. If you are wise, you gather your attention. Attention itself is energy coming back to your spiritual center to help you become stronger. I do not encourage you to become a nun, but I do suggest that you become an example of finding true spiritual benefit; not because of false beliefs, but because you have attained the truth. Men or women can live independently, with internal sufficiency. They can experience adequacy without relying on emotional fantasies.

Q: Here in the Center, women do not need to take on roles any different from the men. We are all just here for spiritual growth. Right?

Master Ni: Right. Women are very influential. In a case where there is a large group and women are in the minority, women have the more important role. If women are the majority, with only a few men, then the men are the influential ones. This is a natural tendency.

Q: It is interesting about the women who come and stay around here. There have been women who come in and then go, but even though we do not think about it, it must take a certain kind of strength to stay and study.

Master Ni: It takes a certain spiritual quality. Some women do not appreciate this kind of activity. What kind of words describe that kind of woman?

Students: Petty, frivolous, not much substance, catty.

Q: For me it has been hard to find friends in Georgia, I have not been able to find women who click with me. Now I am finding that I am more relaxed in my relationships. I

really like some things about some people, maybe not ev-
erything, but I am much more able to take the part I like
about people and not be concerned if everything they do
does not please me or even if it does please me. I find it
easier to accept characteristics of people because I only
have to be with them a short while, not live with them.
They do not have to be my best friend or feel exactly like I
do about everything. It is much more fun to take people
that way. To me, it is enlightening; I see a lot more poten-
tial in the world.

Master Ni: As you say, it is your maturity and your
growth. Do not make trouble for yourself by becoming too
meticulous. In certain circumstances, allow people to live
at your side and live in the same world with you. But do
not be pulled by noisy people.

I think we can let all of your souls peacefully find
their growth in this lifetime. Make all life experience become productive as part of your life process. If you have a
chance to be married, let the marriage be as a team for
spiritual growth and for accomplishing spiritually dedicated work towards helping other people. Some women are
not looking for light, they only wish to attach to someone
or something.

In this meeting, you can clearly see that the position
of women in a study group can be just as influential as
the teacher who gives the material. Without the women's
help, good teaching cannot be correctly realized. Women
have a quiet and clear vision that easily discovers the
impulsive, rash actions or rash expressions of men, who
can easily make mistakes. A man who knows this can let
a woman help keep him from taking action which would
cause him trouble later.

As a woman, you are not going to encourage men to
run into any impulsive action towards you or toward the
world. Always make your work and relationships a process of learning and growing to spiritual maturity for your
spiritual benefit.

I am talking here and your mind understands. Each of you has a soul, a spirit. Your soul, your spirit is also communicating with me. It takes me as its teacher in a way that is much closer and deeper than your body or mind can. Your body and your mind cannot be too close to me, or they would become a different obstacle because of other people's views. Your mind is full of different experiences and obstacles; it cannot fully open, or totally melt together with my mind, into my goal, at this moment.

However, your own spirit, the part before you are born into this world, is there. After you finish your life journey, the body is worn out, the mind is without a brain and not active, but your spirit is still there. You will look for me and find me. The teachers, the real spiritually achieved ones in this tradition, will accept your soul and take care of it. Heaven is our head, Earth is our body, and our free spirit is produced by the intercourse of Heaven and Earth. Let the sun shine internally within your life; you shall find this is the spiritual fruit of your working and living as you go correctly on the way without straying to any side path or being entrapped by unworthy attractions.

So now we close the meeting. I am thankful for this meeting and the beautiful food and tea you have offered.

February 18, 1989
Women's Meeting with Master Ni
At the Center for Taoist Arts, Atlanta, Georgia

Chapter 5

Strength Can be Found Within Oneself

Response from the Women's Meeting:
Part I

Q: This is my reaction to your advice about being non-competitive. I have a friend who is a professional woman. She is divorced from her alcoholic, unemployed husband and has to support three children, one of them handicapped. She cannot afford to accept your concept that women do not have to compete with men.

Master Ni: Rather than being competitive, I teach men and women to become self-strengthening. Competition is external. It is an attitude that reacts to an external challenger. Self-strengthening comes from your inner strength and grows a deep root.

Especially when I talk about women not competing with men, I am talking about women avoiding competing with their husbands inside the home. For example, if both of them try to sleep on the same side of the bed, there will be a fight. Rather than compete or fight, make an agreement.

I am talking about a good relationship assisted by spiritual growth, not a business situation. In business, in work, in school, in a family or any circumstance, I encourage people, all of us, to do self-strengthening, and keep an internal focus rather than concentrate on competition, which brings about tension and suggests improper measure.

In previous books, I may have used the word "competition." I would like to make a distinction between two kinds of competition. There are healthy or honest competition and evil competition. There is nothing at seriously wrong with fair, honest competition; however, sometimes, as you try to keep up with others, it involves a self-sacrifice. It is not having the same spirit and practical measurement of strengthening your own skills in study, work and business, etc. Watch for this and be careful of it. The other type of competition, evil competition, which means using bad measure, even extending to illegal, immoral or underhanded ways to get what you want, is totally incorrect. Absolutely avoid it.

As a society, we cannot go backward. Women want to improve themselves, not regress to their passive role. I work for both men and women. What has happened to women in society during the past 20 years is important. I hope that your new freedoms enable you to use the skill of self-strengthening so that all your needs are met and you feel content in life.

A professional woman who is divorced from her alcoholic, unemployed husband and has to support three children need not compete with anyone to get a job. She should know her strengths and interview for a job with the attitude of doing the best she can. However, to say that she can do a job better than any man, or any other woman for that matter, brings a competitive edge that is disharmonizing and unhealthy.

Student: What advice do you have for a woman who was sexually molested by her stepfather for several years? By the way, one out of four women has been sexually abused as a child.

Master Ni: Yes, it is unfortunate. However, my understanding is that the woman who can take care of herself will not let problems happen. If you have experienced a problem, let go of the anger and resentment so that you can move forward to a positive life for yourself. Women who hang onto the hurts and pains every man ever caused them will not have good lives. Women then need to find a positive way to contribute to the world. If you free up your heart from old hurts, you free up a negative part of yourself and can then go on to spiritual learning.

My answer is not a man's point of view, it is a spiritual point of view.

One of my women students contributed the following as a response to your question:

"The way to free yourself from unpleasant experiences is as follows: 1) (Past) Recognize your past. Do not hide from it. See its reality, then leave it behind you. Do not think about the past. If you do, you relive these experiences over and over again, increasing your own suffering. This includes, if you are angry about something, get over it (do not cry over spilt milk). You cannot change the past. Life has its roughness for everyone, so accept it and move on. You are still alive, anyway. 2) (Present) Find a safe place and a safe way to live your life and take all precaution not to let it happen again. 3) (Future) Change your focus in life from negative to positive by finding any kind of positive, helpful work to do in the world. Find things that bring you happiness, no matter how small. This will give you a rewarding and happy future.

Being quiet and concentrated means to be alert for possible danger and be cautious, do not make yourself a target by being too visible or vocal, and find your own happiness in life rather than relying on anyone else. If someone else (a partner) is there, that is also okay, but you are responsible for the quality of what is in your life.

A teenage girl who is being molested can leave home, get help if she needs it, and then start a new life. It will not be easy, but if she wants it enough, she will do it. I know women that have suffered unspeakable trauma and are victorious in their ability to build good lives for themselves. Each minute and opportunity is new if we do not live in the past, we are cautious in the present and plan for the future."

Whatever happens in your life, it is someone's wrong doing, spiritually. You are involved and you are responsible. So, as a woman you need to not impress men that you are loose, easy to turn on or someone like a man can make you into something he desires. As a woman, you need to have enough sensitivity to know what is in your surroundings and what can maybe happen to you if you become overly self-giving or even just plain nice or friendly to some men. Do not misimpress people or make them get the wrong impression about what kind of woman you are. Spiritual discernment needs to be nurtured. That is important.

Q: How can a woman avoid awkward sexual situations?

Master Ni: Here are several suggestions I wish to give:

1. Establish the understanding of self-protection in sexual matters when you go out with a man or any relative. Do not ever think that a man will protect you. If you trust a man to take care of you and protect you, you are only putting yourself in a vulnerable position.

2. The best self protection is self discipline. Your attitudes about sexual choice must be serious and not loose. Dress properly rather than in a tempting way. In your language, use a tone and show self respect to put a man at a distance. If you respond to others poorly, your words invite trouble for yourself. Do not be afraid to correct your language, manners or anything which has caused a man to have a different impression.

In your private life, if you like things to happen unexpectedly, that will also bring problems.

3. There is no need to fight to express that you are a strong woman, but you need to overcome your own spiritual weakness. If you are insensitive to a situation, you may be tempting men without knowing it. Usually a man will give a subtle signal that he wishes to take you to bed. If you achieve your spiritual quality before such a thing happens or at the time the thing happens, you still have time to correct the situation by withdrawing from it. Thus you will not experience remorse afterward.

Unless you are clear about it being okay to have sexual relations with a certain man, it is better not to get a man interested in the first place than to try to cool him down or walk away from a volatile situation.

4. Sometimes it is easy to prevent a man from taking you to bed, but it is hard to prevent yourself. Many women allow it to happen. They half allow it, consciously or unconsciously. Being willing or partly willing means you are

giving the opportunity or obscure consent to such an experience.

5. It is not hard to know men, it is hard to know yourself. When you are single, if you would like to be undisturbed sexually, you need to know that during ovulation and before and after menstruation are periods of danger or self-entrapment by sexual temptation. At those times, you might easily pick up someone who is not a proper partner. Your greater need to have someone around at those times creates opportunities for self-damage. Protect yourself by finding emotional support during those times, or plan projects so that you are already occupied and do not have time to do something on a whim.

6. In the natural world, male birds and male animals are sometimes more beautiful, like the male peacock and male lion. But in the human world, females are allowed more freedom than men in selection of dress or accessories that make them beautiful. If you would like to look attractive sexually but at the same time you talk about self-protection, you have not attained clarity about what you really want. Instead, you have internal conflict.

Make up and attractive clothing are no defense to keep males from thinking about sleeping with you. Because men's minds are so sensitive, even an exposed neck or leg will cause stimulation. I do not suggest you dress like a nun. Find a balance and dress respectfully and use suitable perfumes, and cosmetics. It is an art to learn how to earn admiration for yourself without causing trouble. Classically styled clothing is always acceptable.

7. In conversation, be careful about who you talk to. If you tell jokes, absolutely avoid sexual stimulation. If you tell sexual jokes, you are educating the man to be excited. He will mistake it as your seduction.

Improper behavior by a man is sometimes a response to the unconscious seduction by a woman. You are not ready to have sex with him, but he is excited by your dress, perfume, and lack of self-discipline.

8. The modern problem is the lack of social morality or family morality. It seems now that people are breaking away from the sense of moral and spiritual responsibility and that even fewer people pay attention to the traditional spiritual knowledge of safe living. We know there is high rate of improper sexual behavior imposed on women by men. However, modern culture conditions society to do this. For example, women are paid to display all kinds of seductive approaches on television, in advertisements and in movies. That conditions men to do things improperly. If you are in a profession that furthers these things, change the focus of your work. Each of us, men and women, are responsible for the cultural quality of the world.

9) In the eyes of men, all young women are like a sweetly smelling flower. If you wear a little dress, it is not a good idea to sit alone with a man. There is no safety unless you are aware of the situation. Withdraw yourself immediately.

10) Unless you are prepared to avoid sexual trouble, avoid walking in the dark. Always travel with safety measures.
    Also be cautious about small things that happen in general. You may pay no attention when an acquaintance or a relative gives you gifts or compliments, you do not see their intention makes it easier for things to happen in the future.

11) A female, whether young girls or adult woman, for self-protection, it is not a good idea to drink alcohol, take drugs or watch a sexual movie together with someone with whom you do not choose to be related. If you do, you give the opportunity to make things happen unexpectedly.

12) Keep the door to your house locked, day and night. Do not open the door unless you know and trust the person who knocks.

Make correct discernment between what does not serve your life and what serves your life. Do not wait for anybody to do anything to stop all the bad conditions. Each person needs to have a correct way of life, proper approach towards all aspects of life. It starts from ourselves. Any external measure is superficial. This is something I would like to point out for your attention.

My suggestions could be insufficient. I asked one of my beautiful woman students who has a successful career in the entertainment business to give her knowledge about self protection:

"When going out at night, always be accompanied by a girlfriend, or someone you know well and trust. Never allow anyone, even if they seem to be in trouble, into your home. You can make a telephone call for them, but keep them outside locked doors.

When driving, do not look around to the cars next to you and smile. (Other drivers may misinterpret the smile.)

Get a post office box mailing address and have an answering service take your phone calls so that no one can trace where you live.

If you car stalls, do not get out of car or roll your window down to talk to anyone who offers to help. Have a heavy marker and paper to write instructions down so that they can call a tow truck, or garage. When another car hits your car, do not get out of your car unless it is absolutely necessary. Try to get the license plate number of the other car from the mirror.

When day is turning to dark, do not stop to talk to anyone. Just walk to your car with the car keys in your hand. If you see or feel someone walking towards you or behind you, put the key ring in the center of your fist with the longest key sticking out between your fore-finger and middle finger. Use this as a weapon."

Another woman student also gave suggestions:

"Work with the thoughts in your mind. By your thoughts, make your own spiritual cultivation more important than anything else. The strength of your focus will help keep you safe, because you will be better able to avoid temptation.

Because Master Ni teaches us that our bodies and our energy are important in spiritual cultivation, treat them as valuables that you need to protect. There must be no reason available in your mind that will give anyone permission to harm you, not even your desire to be a "good person" and help someone. If it threatens your own safety, rather than help someone who was not cautious enough to keep out of trouble, put your own attention to being sure you do not create trouble for yourself.

One woman that I knew had in childhood experienced sexual molestation from her father. She worked on developing herself spiritually and learned how to keep herself safe. These are some of the things she did: 1) She did not go out at night. I often asked her to go to a movie or to visit friends, but she never went if it was in the evening. At first I did not see her wisdom, but now I do. 2) She did not go out in the daytime without a purpose. Spiritually, one leaves oneself unprotected if one does not have a good reason to go out, such as buying groceries or to see someone. Be creative with what you can do with your time and energy at home. You actually might have more enjoyment than if you go out to do something else. And you can cultivate more. 3) Always be sure your car is in excellent working condition so you do not experience trouble. Join an auto club so you will have help if you need it. 4) If you live alone and are afraid of anything, call the police and have them come over to be sure you are safe; it is their job. Even if you think it seems silly, they will come and check things out for you.

Being safe is more important than looking like a silly or foolish woman, a weak or stupid woman, a hysterical woman, a worry wart or "chicken."

If you are interested in a spiritual path, meet or date only men who are on a similar path. Master Ni advises us to beware of spiritual teachers and fellow students who are still weak and unable to face an attractive woman without being pulled away from their original good purpose, or whose original purpose is not pure. Otherwise, you will be diverted from your goal.

As a woman, you must look for the correct situation and environment in which to apply your good nature. If you *apply it incorrectly, you will be victimized, used or abused. So check things out before you give any of your valuable energy and good nature to anything. Guard your body like you guard your money; do not give it to anyone unless you are certain you would like to share it with him."*

American life is going through change. American society is fraught with problems which have only recently been brought to public attention. In the last 20 years, methods have been developed for people to face and cope with these problems (AA, group therapy, journal workshops, family counseling, etc.) These techniques help troubled people begin to become centered and inspire many to look for spiritual harmony. These helps can be recognized as a preliminary step of spiritual learning.

The work of psychological therapists and my work in teaching the Tradition of Tao can go together as different steps to help people. During the last 15 years that I have worked in the West, both psychologists and religious leaders have openly supported and joined my work. Therapists and other group leaders visit the different Centers and refer their clients and group members for further spiritual pursuit.

For example, a couple recovering from the husband's cocaine addiction have preserved their marriage by going for psychological counseling almost daily for six months. Four years later, they are living in harmony. They are beginning to feel the need of further development and are coming to understand that psychological skill brings people only to a certain degree of maturity and achievement. Soon they will begin to pursue deep spiritual learning from my books.

When a couple or any one individual feels they need professional help to overcome a problem or addiction, a psychologist can help them understand basic knowledge. The psychologist can help them further understand themselves and the reason for the addiction or problem. Some people are helped by psychologists or other professionals. It is not a good idea to become dependant upon them. Actually, most people could heal or help themselves without therapy. It is my belief that when you truly desire to overcome anything, you can do it with your own will, and by leading a natural way of life. I have seen people recover from tremendous mental or psychological difficulties without spending a lot of time with psychologists. Retiring to bed early, waking up early, eating healthy food and studying self-help and spiritual books are beginning steps towards a natural life.

Some people can overcome alcohol, tobacco and drugs by their own effort after they understand some spiritual teachings. Most psychological approaches help you to know about the mental level of your problem but they do not always touch your spirit. Because a complete life consists of the three aspects of body, mind and spirit, partial help will not serve the whole individual.

After examining the cause of sexual stimulation in America and understanding its effect, I only can suggest work on oneself. By working to improve your situation, you can guard yourself from possible attack.

If you wish to rely on the policeman or the court of law, it already happened, it is too late. If a woman has suffered from sexual improperness from a man, in the United States she can go to court, but this does not take away the experience. My service can only guide the individual for their own spiritual discipline. It could not correct any event that has already happened. A better future can only be obtained by personal individual spiritual development.

Chapter 6

Clear Choices:
Selective or Minimum Involvement

Response from the Women's Meeting
Part II

In Taoist teaching, what we call cultivation consists of developing a complete life. This includes spiritual life, material life and human relationships. It means we have more work to do than other religions. Some religions declare forsaking worldly life to take care of your peace of mind. Other religions promote going to Heaven, a better place to be after you die, but that is also a single direction and is not broad enough as complete guidance for real, practical life.

In the learning of Tao, you cannot escape any one part of the three aspects. In serious spiritual cultivation, we not only talk about the spiritual and physical sphere, but we also talk about relationships. In spiritual cultivation, there is no discrimination between man and woman. All of us are the same; we each have to face the three spheres of life.

When the Center organized my schedule and included a discussion with women only, that suggested a discussion about relationships. However, I was open to answering questions about whatever the participants wished to discuss.

At this time in modern society, the social position of women is making a new adjustment. This society is changing from being a conventional, male-dominated society and is moving to a new epoch of equality. Change almost always triggers emotion. Those emotions reflect the social struggle of the times. However, social struggle and its related emotion is not Taoist spiritual cultivation. This tradition and I myself do not extend ourselves to political and social issues. We wish to keep our teaching clean and unadulterated so that it is not lost in the turmoil of worldly matters.

Conventional society - please notice I am using the word conventional, not natural - is artificial in the first place, for everybody: men, women and children. The whole social structure of a conventional society is artificial. Through years of effort, many new world leaders in different aspects have already brought about some achievement in continuing to deprogram the old conventional society, especially in the United States. Many leaders of different groups have brought an understanding of social issues to the public's awareness in an attempt to deprogram conventional society. I myself am more interested in spiritual subjects. Although I respect that kind of work, my personal offering is the spiritual knowledge gathered from a natural society. This knowledge has been the focus of the return to natural human life.

Thus, I hope that all of you who participated in the meeting and who read this transcript understand the guideline I give myself. My guideline is a spiritual offering that advises your spiritual growth, but does not fuel your emotion in the social struggle of your half-conventional society. You shall benefit more by studying my spiritual advice and working to understand it rather than focusing on any description that stirs up your emotion.

I do not choose to avoid the real problem without examining it. After having the discussion with my women students, it was mentioned to me that women suffer from men's disrespect. I would like to point out that everybody has a responsibility to help our culture move to a direction which improves our personal life.

Modern life is not centered on the family, but on the economy, which is symbolized by money. Whenever you work for money and exchange your labor for support of your personal life, consider what you do and how it will affect society. It is important for you to make money to support yourself in business, but you must also look at the quality of what you do for a living.

The commerce-centered world stimulates people's desire to spend and enjoy. Sexual motivation appears widely and deeply in all corners of the commercial world. This stimulation encourages you to go to restaurants for gourmet eating and to visit the fashion stores for your fancy styles and but for your emotional satisfaction. Sexual motivation takes people to the cinema where they sit promoting their desires. Things you do more are for your emotional satisfaction. Directly or indirectly you promote the sense of sexual expansion. Then your health is troubled by working hard for spending money and depleting your energy. You need to have constant medical service and live side-by-side with a pharmacy or medical clinic.

The apparent trace of the problem of sexual promotion, if to take section of fact, starts with the fashion shows that are heavy with sexual inducement. The problem can still be traced back to the fashion designers. Those artists need to meet the demand of men and women's taste. Then the development of the whole fashion industry moves to this demand, which drives people for more sexual tendency. To work on and make a living out a direction of business and careers are supported. But all of them probably at least become the smallest element that would condition a criminal behavior of youngsters or misdemeanor. Who else would think about the cultural affect? Nobody thinks about the responsibility of the possible cultural downward suggestion.

People make and spend money. Many businesses, directly or indirectly, are related with sexual promotion. Almost everybody is involved in some way in cultural pollution.

On a nationwide basic, companies that own and manage restaurants where people go to eat and drink for fun and fashion stores, produce movies and TV shoes, and publish sexual books all pay tax to the government. I do not think the government refuses the tax from them. The government uses that money to pay government workers and support social programs, thus, the government is involved in sexual promotion. Do you think priests and churches refuse donations from companies involved in sex-related businesses? They do not. So the church is involved. So are healers and doctors. Everything supports everything, good or bad.

Money was first created to be a symbol of exchange. In a free society, people make money to exchange for their needs.

Money is a symbol for today's living. In Taoist teaching, if you call money "the god of greenness" you should not also call the nervous system "the green god." It means to value your organs, at least no less than money, because the essence of life contains at least four internal elements: physical body, breath, mind, and spirit. The red god stands for the heart, the yellow god stands for the stomach, the black god stands for the kidneys, the white god stands for healthy breathing and the green god stands for the nervous system. Different colors represent different internal needs and desires. You have to look for balance. However, externally, as a young child, you have learned about money. The symbol of money has become the strongest factor that can decide the other aspects of your life. Few people are clear about the distinction between what is the substance of life and what is the tool. The tool is not the goal. Money is merely the instrument. So the way you are brought up in your money culture, with its education and customs, victimizes your mind. At the end, who victimizes you? All people victimize themselves and everybody involved to build a culture that victimizes you.

You do not have to be a victim of your culture nor of yourself. There are choices for individuals living in the modern world. Ancient times are over, are past.

Statistics say that one out of four American women suffers from a bad sexual experience, one out of eight people has AIDS and one out of four Americans die from a heart attack. I do not know whether these statistics are correct or not. However, I do suggest that all people examine their attitudes towards life, themselves and others.

With our personal attitudes, the first important thing in a spiritual life is to be responsible for whatever we do. This change alone, and spiritual cultivation, can change your personal life energy. If your personal life energy changes, your vibration will change. When the vibration of your energy changes internally, then its corresponding external vibration appears as positive changes in your life. In your personal life, you will no longer relate with harmful people.

People do not know they are harmful. They do not think their behavior is harmful, they are only looking for fun or something to do. When you do not have something constructive to do, trouble comes into a life.

Where ever can you find a place where men and women feel safe to stay in the house that does not need a door and the door does not need a lock? You travel anywhere; do you feel it is always safe? Unless you accept the cruel reality of a society, otherwise, freedom attained from minimum involvement shall be the good foundation for our self-development.

All young males are encouraged to have sexual ambition or fantasies. All young men admire pretty women. Do you know how much it costs to support a woman? This involves the sense of money. Positively speaking, to become rich, a man needs to work hard. However, working hard and using the money for careless spending begins a vicious cycle.

The opposite of a rich man is a poor man. One who relies on social welfare, for example, is eating the fruit of someone else's hard work. The person relies on the government. This is not considered virtuous.

On the other hand, the virtuous one works hard and makes money. Thus conversely, the government depends on virtuous people like yourself. Society and all the public structures depend on you. You have to give, because there is a tax on everything. If you do not wish to spend such a large percentage of your income in taxes, government regulations require you to buy luxuries like houses and boats for income tax deductions. You have to buy a big item and get a loan to qualify. So, you buy a car or house to get a loan from a bank. This means you spend money before you make it, but you do it because you need a tax deduction. Your life is mortgaged to someone else. You begin to carry the new type of unnoticeable slavery.

Now, remember, the young man's dream at the beginning was very small: to have a pretty woman. Then he needs to acquire all the material things that meet his ambition.

Spiritually, the external pull of wanting a pretty companion makes him lose his personal spiritual unity, integrity and simplicity. He needs to use all his energy and attention to support the external requirement, therefore his internal life suffers. The casinos feed his emotions, the beverage business is for his stimulation, the soft drinks are for his thirsty mouth. All those businesses make so much money from that the government relies on their taxes to build a strong society.

Government and society need you to spend money. You need to spend so that other people can make money and have something to live on. Advertisers know that sexual images will inspire people to go to restaurants and shops and that they will spend money. However, with the pull of advertisements, you are not yourself anymore. Even if you are not involved with the cultural motivation as described above, you still have taxes. How much from what you make goes to your good life?

Perhaps you would like to skip buying and decide to only pay tax. How the tax money is used is questionable. How much tax money is effectively used for assisting the healthy growth of people and preventing society from becoming damaged externally and internally?

Manufacturing weapons is a business. If you are in the weapons business, you have to find a customer. If you find a customer, you have perhaps made a criminal. Or you sell to small countries. For example, our tax dollars go toward promoting business deals between American arms manufacturers and small countries. What do the small countries buy weapons for? They buy weapons for war and trouble. So how can you expect a peaceful world for yourself and your children? If you start a bonfire to watch other people's houses catch on fire, do not be surprised if your own house goes up in flames, too.

If there were more people who lived a simple and clean life, like myself, immoral or disrespectful businesses would not have any more customers. However, I do not worry about them going hungry, because if they have good business sense, they will merely change the focus of their business to something more moral and still make money.

It is the law of demand that determines what comes on the market, so all customers have to do is change. Then those specific businesses must look for a new direction and there is a possibility for change for the better.

Most businesses, such as soft drinks, publishing, drugs, food, clothing, etc., only provide what meets or satisfies consumer interest and desire. They do not provide the knowledge the consumer needs to make a good choice.

Look at what you feed modern society. The world's trouble is conditioned by people themselves. Each person is involved in giving support. In the ocean, the fish know where to swim to lay eggs, or where to enjoy warmer water in the winter. But in human society, people have even less choice. If you do not like to live in the extreme capitalistic, but free, society, there is another type of extreme: a centrally planned and controlled socialistic society. That is worse. They take everything, including free expression, and do not give you anything.

I have already showed you the picture of how society has become polluted. People are living for life. People are looking for a way to produce money. They will do whatever they can to achieve this purpose. Sometimes people need money for their survival and must do whatever they can even though they know it will be unhealthy for other people or for themselves. Others think they can manipulate the dirty water and improve the world's situation. I suggest one solution. You need your own growth; then you have your own wise choice. You need to better discipline yourself not to feed the pollution.

For example, the air is bad. The air is bad because of the irresponsible industries. The smog of Los Angeles is caused by cars. We all drive cars, so we all create it. The matter of pollution is still measurable or knowable, and how we change our environment depends on our own effort. Do not buy stock in unhealthy products, although they make money, because you are feeding that which is unhealthy. It will come back to destroy not only you, but it will affect your descendants and other people. Make a better choice for a better life, and make money.

I talk about attaining spiritual awareness to stop ourselves from feeding the pond with dirt. Then the fish in the pond will have a better, healthier life. Law cannot have much affect, because it is too external. I can only suggest that each individual discipline oneself and not make the society, culture or atmosphere so lascivious by giving oneself free rein in sexual life. That will motivate men to come back to mistreat women.

Your life mission is to make a serious choice of how to live. Everyone has to accommodate whatever condition of society is present. Self strengthening will enable you to deal with any condition of society. We need to strengthen ourselves not to take the pressure negatively. We need to find our spiritual clarity and make a better choice. We need to extend ourselves to what is healthy and right, and limit our contact with the unclear direction.

Few people can declare that they have not been victimized by the unhealthy trend of time and society. It may not be possible to totally avoid it, but at least we can try to minimize the situation.

In Taoist teaching, we have found the secret to riding time and society. To do that, we need to remember the principle of balance. This means not to be totally pulled out and also not be too inward or selfish to any great extreme. Neither is the healthy way to live. We must look for balance in our lives.

It is necessary to accommodate a good situation of the positive aspect of society, the necessities of our lives, and some good social customs, etc. However, do not become involved with, even look at, or be pulled down by the negative aspects of the society. It affects all of us to a certain depth. You do what you can to help, but if you cannot bring progress to a certain darkness in the world, continuing to look and talk about it can damage yourself spiritually, mentally, and emotionally. Mostly, you need to learn to use external situations to find and accomplish your spiritual essence of life and to grow the internal sweetness which is life's real reward.

I also talk about not feeding the culture. Not making the culture bad is also part of our responsibility. Mediums of communication, such as newspapers and television, are especially influential to people's minds. It is alright if they report criminal behavior, but they do not need to describe the details. Giving the details teaches people of undeveloped mind how to fulfill criminal behavior. People are so affected by what they see or hear, so if you work in those mediums of communication, I suggest you help improve them. Let me give you an example of how newspapers can affect a person.

Taiwan was originally an agricultural society. During the latter part of my 27 year stay in Taiwan, the country was slowly changing from being an agricultural society to a highly developed industrial and commercial society.

Around 15 years before I left Taiwan, in 1960, the first murder case happened in Taiwan. A man killed his ex-wife, cut her body into pieces, put it into a briefcase, and threw the briefcase into a city water ditch. This was the first murder case on the peaceful island; at least, no big thing had happened before in that society. Or through Taiwan's whole history, nothing like that had been reported.

How did it happen? The man had divorced his wife but still stayed with her. He had no job and felt psychologically impotent. The woman brought another man into the house, and they slept together in a room. During that six months, the ex-husband grew hatred in his mind that got stronger every day. He did not find a way to express or deal with his hatred.

At that time, Taiwan was not as developed as it is today. Some people were poor and lived in illegal shacks in government land by the roadside. They used boards for walls, a tent for the roof, and old newspapers to keep the cold air from getting in the cracks. One such newspaper had been used to ship merchandise to Taiwan from Japan. In it, a man described a murder case in Tokyo. Because Japanese characters were developed from Chinese characters, they are fairly easy to read by a Chinese reader. A person can read part and develop a little bit to know the whole story. It turned out that the murder the man accomplished was almost the same as the one described in the newspaper that was in the wall of his house. The man was inspired and taught by that old newspaper.

To help keep the world from getting worse, people who work in the field of communication would do best to keep their work in a healthy direction. I do not say that everybody can make a living in the same way, but we can make a healthy living, and not feed the darkness or make the culture dirty. If you do, then in the future, that type of thing will come back to punish you yourself, your wife, children or descendants. People of spiritual awareness know this.

We do not expect society to be organized tightly with central control, such as a communist society. This was seen during the first thirty years of communism in China. There is no advertisement at all. The criminal rate is less but the activity of commercial health is suffocated and the organic condition of human society was destroyed. So it depends upon ourselves, people who live in a free society, to be correct by correct choice, not by external discipline of some one's narrow design.

All things, healthy or unhealthy, influence others. I and my family are working on spreading health because we hope it can become an important part of American life. I do not calculate or estimate whether any good result will be brought about, but we do it. At least my family and my good students work in that direction.

Today's problems belong to both women and men. Men are children of women. Women are daughters of men. Please pay attention to bringing your sons and daughters up correctly so they will not harm one another.

Although the facts of worldly life are not encouraging, the one encouraging direction for each individual is to look for enlightenment in your life and for spiritual development. That is what we call the path or Tao. To learn Tao, basically, is to learn a healthy life. I have written a set of books about this.

Q: Dear Master Ni, when you talk about external society too much, especially about the conflict and trouble, it pulls me down and gives me a headache. I really wish that you would talk about cultivation, or write poems about oneness. That will keep my mind going in the right direction and will keep me feeling oneness within myself rather than feeling troubled. I do not want to feel troubled by seeing the picture of this type of problem in this talk. I want a reminder of the spiritual unity I am looking for.

Master Ni: All societies have two sides: the positive and the negative. Even a good society, in a good time, still has a small negative corner. We are happy to live in a free society. Thus, we can make our spiritual and mental adjustment with this privilege.

As I have mentioned, we learn to live in the world. We need to learn to accommodate the external social environment, but we cannot give up our spiritual awareness and spiritual responsibility for society. It is not effective to become one of the mob yelling in the streets. Yet, it is not moral to reject someone who is protesting something that is wrong.

Can society really produce the wise, balanced leaders to improve the world? All the political, financial, and religious leaders were children who grew up in the mud. They know only the mud, even thought they may have learned to do better. Those among them who have a strong conscience, might still cherish the hope to be able to clean up the mud.

The only good step you can take is to start from the extension of your own spirit, and help others live a healthy life. Do some good work, and do not just look around and demand that someone help. To live a worthy life is to see how much help we can give in our spare time to general society.

I have mentioned that responsibility to build a good citizen starts from the family. Good fathers and mothers are individuals who are prepared financially and spiritually to be parents. In a natural society, the family is the center of society. Family discipline rests on both the father and the mother. Parents need to pay attention to the growth of their children. If people's focus helps only their own children, this help is still limited. People need to help other people's children as well, because children go to school and into society and learn from each other and other people.

You cannot expect a politician to bring any goodness to the world. Most politicians, like everyone else, are people of circumstance, also conditioned by society. Upright statesmen work hard and wish to benefit the world. However, what each one of them does is limited.

The depth of possible help is our own balanced way of life. It is discouraging to see others suffer by being split in spiritual, psychological, emotional levels. Yet, we must take care of ourselves and start a clean way of life.

Chapter 7

Questions on Spiritual Issues

Q: Master Ni, I have been told that a person should not kill or eat meat because it is immoral and not spiritual to take a life. What does your tradition hold about that question?

Master Ni: This is an issue often brought up to spiritual people by students who have experienced the teachings of other eastern religions. Should people kill? The question is, should people hunt and kill animals for meat and so forth?

My answer is that if you have enough spiritual sensitivity, you will consider this question and be able to make your own decision. People go to school for a long time, take jobs and engage in all kinds of endeavors because they wish to have a good life. Basically, people are looking for survival; nobody can deny that, except perhaps a person born with a silver spoon in his mouth, and that also has a pertinent effect on his life.

In our survival attempts, we make all sorts of efforts, adjustments, adaptations and compromises. Our life itself is looking for life; the instinct of life is to look for life. All animals have the same deep nature of looking for survival. So, in this natural current of survival, is it right to kill other animals? I would say no, with one exception, and that is if an animal is endangering or harming your survival; then you have a reason to apply the killing energy. Otherwise, you do not have the natural right. Humans only have the right to be master over the livestock they raise. Why? Because those animals have lost the sense of survival. Unless a wild animal is making trouble, we do not have the right to kill it. This is the basic practice. We can buy meat at the store, so we do not need to kill animals for our food.

Look at ants. They work hard. I think they work harder than any humans, except perhaps Chinese farmers. Bees work hard too. Basically, it is nature looking for life, looking for survival. We do not have the right to kill ants. Because we are humans, we are giants to them. We could destroy them easily, but we should not. Unless, for example, there are ants in your kitchen or on your dining table; then you need to do something to get rid of them. That is different. When I was first invited to the United States, some of my American students had a background in Buddhism. They saw me with a fly swatter in the kitchen, killing flies. They were startled. How could a spiritual teacher kill a fly? Well, I do. I am a different kind of teacher. I do not allow unhealthy things to partake of my meal before I eat.

There were some Buddhist masters, for example, who went their whole lives without changing clothes; there were thousands of fleas in their garments. In that spiritual practice, they offered their blood as life to those insects. Another Buddhist monk went to Burma where there is a magnificent Buddhist pagoda. The monk worshipped at the pagoda, but at nighttime he would sleep in a trench to allow the mosquitos to feed on him. People in these two examples are looking for that kind of practice. It is probable that they wish to extend their kindness even to insects. What is the true purpose that this type of kindness serves? I think a human life can be spent more meaningfully than by feeding insects; a human life can accomplish something more valuable than that.

However, in Buddhism, the first commandment is no violence. On the surface, the words seem like the teaching of Lao Tzu, but Buddhism developed some views from the practices of Jainism, so a different meaning is suggested. The basic faith of Jainism says that every life has a spirit. The followers of Jainism do not even dare walk on the unswept ground; they are afraid they might kill an insect or trample the blades of grass. Well, if you live in the world, you need a certain amount of spiritual sensitivity but you also need to have spiritual knowledge about what is suitable to do and what is not suitable to do.

Maybe I say this because I am from a different discipline from them. Some of this is my personal advice; people should do whatever is appropriate according to the stage of their understanding.

Q: Master Ni, I feel this brings up another question: abortion. This issue is under great debate in public, in the states and in the courts. What is the viewpoint of the tradition of Tao?

Master Ni: On many occasions, I have talked about how in the learning of Tao, the ancient developed ones evolved skills and formulas for birth control. They looked to obviate the problem before a life was formed. After a certain stage of life has been formed, and if there is no truly good reason, a person had better not have an abortion. A being that comes to the mother and father has received the opportunity to return to the world, whatever the spiritual background of the new life.

As a teacher, students often call on me about such a decision, including married couples and people who live together. It is really hard for me to say anything, because it involves the spiritual responsibility for killing an innocent. Because I practiced Taoist medicine, one of my T'ai Chi students once came to my clinic with his pregnant wife. They wanted an abortion. He was a devoted student and surely I knew how to accomplish it, but I did not. My refusal disappointed the student; he thought that I was being unfriendly. After that, he became detached from the class. I felt sorry for that, but not deeply sorry, because I knew that I had made the correct decision.

On another occasion, a husband and wife let me study their birth charts. They were spiritually devoted and they already had two children. My principle is to never to suggest abortion, but from a reading of their birth charts, it was apparent there would be no beneficial children. I mentioned that out of giving earnest service. However, they chose the possible alternative I indirectly mentioned and resolved the pregnancy through abortion. I felt spiritually sorry for that.

It was a service that I gave to that particular student and if it happened on an occasion in a general situation, I would still say it. But it was a coincidence that the person who was already pregnant used the information; what I told them more or less had an influence. That means I have some responsibility. Therefore, I advise all my friends to practice birth control rather than have an abortion after becoming pregnant. If they do choose abortion, then it needs to be done very early, in the early weeks. Later, artificial abortion is worse and can harm a woman's health.

As students of the immortals, we might like to ask ourselves, what does immortal mean? Apparently, it means survival; spiritual survival without form after the formed life. How can anyone deny another's natural opportunity for survival? One must be very careful.

Nature itself, through many forms, creates life to express life energy. We had really better avoid harming the survival, the life opportunity, of other lives.

Q: Master Ni, should spiritual people be married? I love and care for someone very much.

Master Ni: My typical answer is that, if the couple is together for the purpose of having children, they should be married. In that way, they can offer financial and psycho-logical stability to the children, for at least twenty years. That length of time is chosen to avoid causing any psycho-logical problem for the child so that he or she can become a healthy citizen, the future master of the world. If it is not done for the purpose of raising children, marriage for some people is only a certificate, a piece of paper, a formality. I do not think the certificate is more important than true harmony, true rapport and true affection between man and woman.

Q: But Master Ni, doesn't that give a man an excuse to just stay with a woman until he feels like doing something else, and then leave her on a whim? That indicates lack of responsibility to me. Also, I know many wives who worked for years to put their husbands through school, etc., and then after the man became successful, he left his helpful wife for someone new.

Master Ni: I think for the woman of today spiritual develop-ment is important, in order that she understand about the investment of her love and life. The limited secondary answer to this question is that a man should compensate a woman after having a relationship with her. Normally no woman would accept that. No educated woman would allow her body to be commercialized. Basically, it is a question turning around how strong the man is financially and how affectionate he is towards the woman. A strong man sometimes tends to use women to satisfy his own physical desires out of a lack of consideration. There can be some work done in exchange, so the man gives some work and payment, or does some kind of service in exchange. If the man is my student, after my saying this, he should understand; if possible, he can reflect to see how he can help the woman get along on her own. This may mean financial support, social assistance or some other kind of assistance. It does not matter if we have the seal of a marriage certificate or if it is a natural attraction. What matters is your personal spiritual sensitivity and your consideration.

A woman is not like a paper cup - to be thrown in the garbage after you use it for a drink. A man cannot employ that kind of attitude towards women. I do not say that the ancient type of protective knight needs to be revived in today's society. Spiritually we need to say, more or less, we take care of the weak and needy. If we have that strength, how can we take advantage of people weaker than we are? Surely, it also depends on how well you get along.

Spiritual people cannot owe anybody anything. In different circumstances, if you cannot directly repay back a favor to the person who granted it, you must pay the favor to somebody else, the general public or unknown people. This is basic. It is too hard to talk about virtuous fulfillment, but at least a person can be clean, spiritually pure. It is important for your soul.

Q: In my life and cultivation, in my relationships and my work, your teachings have given me much guidance. I wonder if there is a good illustration to sum up what is the most important in our learning. Would you help us?

Master Ni: I have talked about being natural and original; in other words, it means being proper and suitable in a situation. This is not the way of life among most adults, because of the influence of the popular culture, newspapers, magazines, movies and television.

It was my own experience when I was young to have learned Tao. To help me attain a good understanding, my father let me use his whole collection of books; he encouraged me to read widely from many important works. Also, if achieved teachers came to visit who were also his friends, I was at their side serving tea, so I listened to their discussions and I was inspired by that.

But the most significant work my father asked me to do was to refine the immortal medicine. I am talking about external immortal medicine here, not internal. A portion of the product was used for his patients. In ancient times, this was done on a stove. Today, you can turn the knob on a stove and the flame will immediately start. You can easily control the modern appliance to produce a flame that is large or small and you have the whole range of equipment in a modern pharmaceutical laboratory. Back then, stoves were not like that. To refine such medicine we used a stove, similar to but not the same as the ordinary charcoal stove used at that time. To cook food, people used all kinds of charcoal, but to refine the external immortal medicine, instead of charcoal they used a wood which produced the desired heat and which had spiritual meaning, too. All kinds of fragrant, good wood was used to start and maintain the fire in that stove.

On top of the fire, a specially made earthen jar was placed. It was slim and tall; on the inside of the lip, we took the crystal essence that gathered from the medicine in the bottom of the pot.

I was the one assigned to take care of the fire. I had to use a small fan to keep the fire going, and continually fed the stove with the wood charcoal. You see, because the stoves were not mechanical, a young man had to learn how to exercise his mind to control the fire. The demand of the temperature and size of the fire was required to be precise for the process to work. Controlling the small, medium or large fire was important. It was not hard to control it as you desire. It is hard to keep it constantly as a small fire, medium fire or high fire.

It was a matter of persisting with the fire for seven days or forty nine days. All that time, the temperature could not change if the condition in the pot were to produce the desired medicine. The hard part was that you could not sleep if you felt drowsy; if you did, the fire would immediately change. If the fire was too hot, it would burn the material inside. If the fire was too cool, the refining process would cease. So it needed to be maintained at a certain degree, not mechanically, but by your watching it. That is your great control. It was great training for a young boy. I worked for my father doing that.

That training made me understand that sometimes we are too hot and sometimes we are too cold. By being too hot or too cold, we spoil the immortal medicine of our life. A person can spoil his or her life, a relationship, a job situation, prosperity, whatever, by moving the mind away and thus neglecting the situation being faced. If only one thought happens to occupy the mind, we may not recognize it, but the internal situation changes, and even with one small external change, the medicine inside the pot could be spoiled or not crystallize as we expected.

My father used the medicine for cancer patients and for all kinds of serious diseases, what was left over was used as ordinary medicine. That immortal medicine was to assist old people; young people have no need of it.

The high meaning, I believe, of my father asking me to do that, came from two very practical reasons. One, I was the young man who took care of and watched the fire for 7 or 49 days without the fire changing for one second. That needs a great deal of patience, which I lacked, though my father frequently came to help me. The second thing was that many times I had the impulse to open the lid of the jar to see what was happening inside. But I stopped myself from doing it. Although I really wanted to hurry up the result, it could not be hurried. This requires rational strength with which to control one's impulse. So that was the meaningful training.

The immortal medicine made in that earthen pot is not the same kind that I have mentioned in my books, the internal immortal medicine; the latter is an analogy to the process I have just described.

As I have emphasized to you, one aspect of immortality is training to control our temperatures, whether young or old, and to learn to manage our psychological and emotional fluctuations. When we do not, we often spoil our lives and spoil our good internal conditions. We are born immortal, but unfortunately, much of the time we spoil ourselves. By being either too hot or too cold, we lose the suitability and fitness for an enduring life.

During the long refinement process, you cannot sleep; you need to put yourself in a type of meditative self-centeredness. You adjust the fire outside on the stove and inside you adjust the internal fire of keeping awake. The keeping-awake strength is the same thing as the fire. It is not only external adjustment, it is primarily internal adjustment. It is also not being wholly awake. You eat, you watch and you do everything at the side of the stove.

I do not know if you have the image of an earthen stove, with open space in front, set up in a beautiful, quiet place. You use your fan to encourage the flame. There should be no wind nor any other disturbance. It is started after determining the most auspicious day. In the beginning, and during the process, you make offerings to the spiritual realm to assure the success of the refinement.

To me, the refinement is an example of spiritual training. It is the spirit of sublimity, integrity, high sincerity and good concentration. Many times I use the word "self-refinement" in my teaching of Tao; it is from the image and experience of that training. That type of work is called refinement. I recommend that people understand how we can maintain our own spirit from that example.

Chapter 8

Truthful Love Comes
From a Balanced Mind

*Commentary from the Book of Changes and the Unchanging
Truth, Hexagram 31*

The mutual response of two young hearts presents the
picture of love. This is illustrated by ☱ a young girl, and
☶ a young boy, and the mutual attraction shared
between them.
When I was young, I focused more on my spiritual
achievement than on experiences of love. After studying the
important teachings of the three main cultural traditions -
Taoism, Confucianism and Buddhism - I harmonized and
expressed all three with the following words:

> *"Confucianism is my garment,*
> *Buddhism is my cane and*
> *Taoism is my sandal."*

My young, proud mind seemed to be satisfied with this
combination. However, one day I discovered that someone
had added some new, handwritten words to each line of my
writing on the wall of my study. These lines now said:

> "Confucianism is my garment,
> - *it is too short for you!*
> Buddhism is my cane,
> - *it is too weak to support you!*
> and Taoism is my sandal
> - *it has been worn out long ago!"*

My first response to this discovery was outrage. I
thought it must be my younger brother or elder sister
making fun of me, but since it did not seem to be an ordinary joke, I immediately corrected my judgment. The person
who wrote these lines had to have a vision higher than, or
equal to, mine. I felt puzzled. Who could have done this?

Since the handwriting was not much better than mine, it could not be the work of a dignified adult. Also, this happened to be my personal study upstairs. I was the only one who used most of the upstairs rooms, except for the one used as the family shrine. After making many inquiries of my family, I discovered that some of my sister's girlfriends had visited us. One of them had been in our family shrine for a short while. She was the only daughter of one of my father's friends. She had to be the one who did this. She was famous for being the most beautiful girl in our town. She was also well-educated and a lover of literature.

Although I had never paid attention to her before, I decided I must pay her a visit. I thought of the ancient one's saying: "Three people are walking together; one of them must have something I can learn." I dressed myself neatly and directly went to see her.

She received me in the small hall of their garden. After our greeting, I politely and straightforwardly requested an explanation of the addition I was certain she had made on my study wall. She flushed and suggested that if I would call on her for ten days she would then give me her explanation. I agreed to this as my respectful lesson. Thus, every afternoon I went to her house. We read some good, ancient poetry, played Chinese chess and did some gardening. Our friendship developed more with each day. When she tenderly touched the back of my hand, I felt that something had struck me, yet I liked it. Her eyes were the most beautiful poem I had ever read. The sweetness of her delicate smell intoxicated me. Her smile engulfed me.

Before long, however, a difficulty surfaced in our budding romance. It appeared that she was especially attached to a novel entitled *The Red Chamber*. I could never agree with her belief that *The Red Chamber* held the truth of life and, likewise, she could never agree with my Kung Fu practice.

When we reached the end of our ten-day period together, I again requested her explanation of the lines she had written on my wall. She asked for my palm, upon which she wrote a Chinese character with her gentle, slim finger. The Chinese word struck me in the same way I was struck by her finger, moving lightly over my palm. It was the character for the word "love" or, more appropriately in this case, "affection."

Now I was even more bewildered than before. I could not refrain from asking her what connection could possibly exist between the love of which she spoke and her addition to my writing. At first she hesitated. Then finally, with apparent difficulty, she said, "You like to think very much of Confucianism, Buddhism and Taoism, but without the word 'love' nothing has any meaning in life. Have you ever thought of that?"

This was a real question for me. Since I had never experienced love, I had never truly pondered this question. I answered frankly, "I do not know yet. How do you know?"

"From *The Red Chamber*," she answered.

I frowned. I had read the book and did not like it. When I told her that, she responded, "What is wrong with a girl and a boy falling in love as described in that book?"

"I don't know. It seems like too much trouble to become involved in such complicated love," I replied.

"Well, it seems to me like Confucianism, Buddhism and Taoism give you even more trouble with all kinds of study and discipline," she argued.

"I haven't thought about that. However, you have given me your explanation. I shall now go home to discover, through my own cultivation, the true significance of that word."

Though it was time to say good-bye, her eyes kept staring into mine and I felt their warmth flow into my body. Gradually, her eyes became moistened, tears falling from them like a string of pearls. I did not know how to help her. After a long while with her handkerchief to her face, she said, "You are always contemptuous toward me and the other girls. You will not come to see me again."

"I don't know. I'll think about it," I replied.

"It will be too late to see me if you only think about it. I shall die only for love, like Blue Jade (the main female character in *The Red Chamber*). Can you understand?" she asked.

"I shall go home and study this book that you like so much."

She offered, "I would like for you to have my copy since it is the best version." She went into her inner room to get the copy of her "holy book" and gave it to me. I took the book and left.

Though we had several versions of *The Red Chamber* in our house, I had never been able to read through any one of them in its entirety. The main story described the life of Precious Jade, a young man of a noble and wealthy family. Although his youth was spent in an elegant garden with many beautiful girls as his companions, he fell in love only with Blue Jade. However, his family arranged for him to marry a girl for whom he had no love. Soon afterward, Blue Jade died from her disappointment in love. Precious Jade's family also suffered decline. Precious Jade himself discovered that his entire life was but an empty dream and thus decided to leave the dusty world to become a Buddhist monk.

Though this book was a good work of literature, the love it described was very narrow. I could not recognize any high truth with which the author could illuminate human life. However, since I wanted to be with my friend and because I still felt difficulty with the question of love, I turned to my mother for help.

My mother told me, "An ancient sage once said, 'Even a developed one feels trouble communicating with women and children.' Problems are created when people of different levels of development come together. Therefore, spiritual development sometimes makes it more difficult to be with ordinary people. If this shortcoming of a developed person is not moderated, it can bring extreme isolation to him. This would not be a very beneficial direction for anyone to go in, unless it is done so intentionally, with a positive purpose for some special cultivation.

"Love is a very important matter in life. Nobody can ignore it. In general, as you already know, love can be classified into two different categories: broad love and narrow love. Broad love is humanistic, and all the ancient sages were recognized for their broad love. Confucius (551-

416 B.C.) and Mencius (372-298 B.C.) exalted humanistic love. Mo Tzu (501-479 B.C.) exalted universal love and made himself as a model to realize it. He led a life of absolute self-abnegation. He exerted himself to the fullest extent of his life by working for the peace of humanity. Lao Tzu valued natural impartial love as the highest level. Sakyamuni exalted compassion and equal love. In general, humanistic love is developed, peaceful, impersonal and dispassionate love. This is what human nature was born with and what human beings should continue to cultivate. Also, in general, narrow love can only be practiced between two people, like a boy and a girl, a man and a woman, a husband and wife, or among a group of people like a family, a circle of friends, a religious fellowship, a society, a nation or a race.

"The practice of narrow love is usually passionate. Passion is what makes love narrow. Passionate love can be a good experience during one's youth, but passion needs to be well-guided and controlled. Although the emotional experience of narrow love can be beautiful, it can also be harmful. Broad, humanistic or natural love, however, can be enjoyed throughout this life and all lives. Whether love is humanistic or passionate, it always needs to be guided by the principle of balance. If one loses his balance in the name of love, then that way of loving is unhealthy.

"All people are born with passion, yet different patterns of passion give people different temperaments. One's temperament is influenced by all the stages of one's pre-natal and postnatal life. Parents must take the great responsibility to smooth their own temperaments when raising children in their pre-natal and post-natal stages. An individual must also take responsibility to cultivate himself and regulate his own temperament when a certain level of growth is reached, or as the saying goes, 'An adult must take responsibility for his own ugly face.'

"Now we come to the matter of adjusting one's personal temperament. One's temperament is like one's dog: one needs to put a muzzle and leash on it when taking it in public. Surely achievement comes when one has cast off one's 'dog' nature which is molded by the environment.

"Passion is natural. It is something we are born with, but the way we express our passion is a matter of our environment. We develop that expression ourselves, thus it is controllable and reformable.

"Passion is like water. Water is always water, but in its different phases, the speed and shape of its flow vary greatly. It can be a swift current, a big flood or a torrent. It can be slow moving, or stagnant and motionless. It can also be a rising or ebbing tide, overflowing or draining a stream, lake, ravine, river or ocean. When water meets heat, it becomes vapor; when it meets cold, it becomes ice. Dew, rain, hail, fog, frost, ice, snow and so forth, all come from water. The water always remains the same - it is the environment which causes its different characteristics. Passion is like that.

"Passion is only a part of the whole human mental being, however. There is still the higher sphere of the mind which needs to be cultivated and developed so that one can have good control over the passion of the lower sphere of the mind. A raft riding the torrents cannot carry many people. Danger may be lurking anywhere along the journey's path. Though one may enjoy the excitement of riding a raft in the torrents, this is not a normal, everyday practice. If one's passion is like a torrent, then one's life is like a raft. How dangerous that is! How long can the enjoyment of such excitement last? Is it worth exhausting one's life? This seems to be a poor model of normal, healthy passion.

"Love is a beautiful passion; however, when emotional force or possessiveness is attached to what one loves, the sublime state of pure love is degraded or damaged. Surely, a spiritually developed person can still feel personal love, but it is unattached and unoccupying love. This is the fine quality of true spiritual love. The nature of spiritual love is subtle. One can unceasingly appreciate beauty without creating the troubles which accompany its ownership. Therefore, a full life of appreciation can be lived without carrying the weight of worldly burdens.

"Out of one's humanistic love comes the courage to accept responsibility for the world. This is certainly not a rigid practice. Most ancient Taoists, if not living in the high mountains married to the beauty of nature, would travel around the world like a white cloud flying across the sky. Nothing could restrict them.

"The particular practice of love in our family is to reach the level of the ancient Taoists. We follow the external patterns of secular life, but within this everyday life we fulfill the broadness of spirituality. In other words, we use the roughness of the world and the difficulties of practical life as the friction that creates our spiritual sparks. This is what people call enlightenment or inspiration. Although enlightenment and inspiration are only momentary experiences, they can mark where one has reached. Furthermore, the endurance of life, which is built from the difficulties of worldly life, is our actual realization of universal, impartial love. The refinement of one's passions and emotions becomes an important aspect in this realization.

"Some people cannot see with their partial vision that the truth is total. They think there can be no existence of individual happiness in the practice of humanistic love, but the real truth is that individual happiness exists only in the happiness of its completeness. Can one have happiness when the entire world suffers from a flood? One can only fulfill one's own life through the harmonious fulfillment of all lives. That is why, in our family, we live for ourselves as well as for the entire world, with a clear spiritual direction."

Then my mother continued, "In the narrow sense of a family, your father is our life-maker. I am the home-maker and also a life-maker. We are all makers of a common life. We fulfill our individual duty and also assist the fulfillment of each other's duty. I am sixteen years younger than your father. I respect and love him and he has much tolerance and understanding toward me. Actually, he treats the entire world this same way, but I am the one who has the blessing to live with him. Furthermore, your father is a man of spiritual development, thus our love is mainly spiritual rather than physical. Being spiritually linked is the source of our happiness.

"If love is true, the experience of love and deep joy occur in the same moment. It is not joyful to reminisce about a particular moment of love in the past. The enlightenment of love exists in each moment. There is no search that can find love, nor any occasion that can create love. You know love when your heart is open. The music is silent, but its harmony pervades your entire being. In that moment there is no separation.

"Love is the golden light of the sun rising within your being. It is the rose which has just opened its eyes. It is the freshness of dew or the caress of a wave on the shore - all within you.

"But the dawn becomes noon and finally evening. The early morning dew evaporates. The rose reaches its fullness and its petals fall. A wave reaches its crest and returns to the sea. Then, does love also die? If the love within us is living, does it also die when it reaches its fullness? Can one hold that certain moment of the sun's first appearance on the horizon? Can one make love endure? At what point does the joy of love's presence become the need for its possession? When one fears it will go away or die is when the need for its possession arises. At this point love becomes contaminated with emotion and need, and its original harmony changes to dissonance. Love then reverts to the realm of duality, and the presence of Tao within our hearts is missed.

"Love can be fulfilled without becoming trapped in the web of emotional needs. We can learn from the virtue of a well which exists for all to take from. Its spring never runs dry. When our inner treasure is inexhaustible, we can provide limitless love and still remain independent and non-possessing.

"In our tradition, we can enjoy the sunrise within us every moment. Our love is as free as the blowing wind and as enduring as a flowing river. Since we continually renew ourselves, we do not fear losing love. Our cultivation becomes our lover, for our love is Tao. Thus, love never withers, for it is continually refreshed.

"When the time comes that you feel love for someone, be gentle. Love has a delicate nature. Never be rough with it or it will be completely destroyed. Always distinguish the difference between love and desire. Love gives pleasure; desire creates pressure. Desire, loneliness, tension and disappointment can all deteriorate the delicate nature of true love. To love is to be gentle. Tender love is truly beneficial in any circumstance. If love is not given gently, it becomes stormy. Stormy love, like stormy weather, can never last long. Generally this kind of love comes out of an imbalance in one's personality or from the pressures of an unhealthy environment.

"Young people may say tender love is weak love, but this is not true. Motherly love is tender love. An eagle soars in the sky and finds its prey among a group of small chickens searching for food in a meadow. It quickly dives to the ground, but before it can extend its sharp claws to capture its prey, the weak old mother hen has already spread her wings and gathered all her chicks under them. She puts herself, face to face, in confrontation with the aggressor. Love can give birth to courage and courage can subdue the strong. You have witnessed this great scene many times in our country life.

"I always tell your sisters that marriage is for happiness. A woman must learn to avoid emotional competition and confrontation with her man inside the house and understand that some men do not like to have another 'manly' person in his private life. I also tell your sisters to be responsible in family life, but not bossy over anyone. In a man's world, there may be already enough bosses in his life outside the family. It is not difficult for a woman to earn love and respect from a man by being tender and by being faithful, not by fighting or competing.

"You feel troubled about correctly responding to the love that comes from this good girl. You can love her if it is your true response. This might be the first time you sail the oceans of love. However, there is nothing to be afraid of. When the current becomes rough, keep yourself centered as usual, and get complete control of your ship. As far as I can see, this girl is not a torrential type of girl. She is more like the beautiful flow of a brooklet; the poetic feeling of her presence can calmly be absorbed.

"However, do not develop your young spiritual love into sentimental love. The love of Precious Jade and Blue Jade is not a good example of pure love. It is not healthy to imitate it. Healthy love bears the fruit of deep rejoicing; nothing can alter it and nothing can be exchanged for it. The beauty of sentimental love can earn wide appreciation on a literary level. However, if it occurs in practical life, it must be the result of an emotional imbalance or feelings of insecurity. Above all, such imaginary love lasts for only a short time. Her imitation of Blue Jade should not be encouraged by you through helping her all day to prepare a funeral for the fallen flower petals and then helping her bury them while singing the funeral hymn. I heard she has been doing this already for years. This is a silly matter, and it is ominous to accept the suggested destiny of Blue Jade in *The Red Chamber*.

"The challenge she makes on your young spiritual authority will surely benefit you. Remember, never be bothered about those who speak or write better than you. Always be mindful of achieving your own transpiercing vision of reality. She has not developed higher than you. Her motivation could be the need for your love. Now, restore your inner balance and give her an answer."

The same day, I wrote my answer to her and returned her copy of *The Red Chamber*. The following is what I wrote:

> "Confucianism is my garment,
> - it is too short for me.
> Buddhism is my cane,
> - it is too weak to support me.
> Now I become a worshipper of The Red Chamber.
>
> I am going to help Precious Jade secularize
> from his tedious life as a monk.
> I am going to revive his Blue Jade
> with my Taoist Magic."

Many modern people have broken off any contact with conventional cultural and spiritual influence because of the new way of life. This is because modern people are more intellectually developed than their ancestors. The modern intellectual mind finds it hard to accept the old way of speaking which was based on the less intellectually developed mind. If you can let pass those teachings that lack real intellectual strength, the spirit behind the childish talking of old religions was the true spirit as the human culture. I mean that it is not right to ask you to attack the old interpretation but directly reach for the spirit. It is some work for intellectually minded people to learn to understand the simplistic speech of the old religions. Behind the child-like talk shines the real spirituality. This is the forever direction of human culture. My mother's teaching was for people who live their lives under a manageable situation. It is not a sudden response when someone experiences rough situations.

We can let the old ways of speaking die off. However, the spirit of human culture cannot die, although it was tested many times by the barbaric trend of some human leaders and their followers in different generations. Howev-er, it is our responsibility to rekindle the spirit of gentle culture.

In the *Tao Teh Ching*, Lao Tzu taught that softness can overcome hardness and tenderness can overcome rough-ness. That is the only correct direction of human culture and spirit. It is hard to apply this to the outside world; only a few wise ones can do that. It is much more useful to establish gentle communication in society and in the family than to try to use your gentleness to improve the rough world at specific occasions. Gentle communication is the foundation of a family. Gentle communication is spiritual guidance or teaching.

In normal family life, women are not usually physically stronger than men. Then, how can a woman can tame the roughness and harshness of a man? By her tenderness and gentleness.

If a woman is emotionally uncontrolled, she easily reacts roughly or as strongly as men do. Then, she spoils the happiness she wishes to have in married life. Men do not always know about the strength of gentleness in family life because worldly life conditions them to become rough and hard. The men only become gentle if they are wise, aware of a situation and able to correct their attitudes. A woman may seem to be in an uneasy position because she is physically weaker. However, one of the best ways to deal with a man's roughness and crudeness is to observe it and avoid it. If hardness reacts to hardness, and roughness reacts to roughness, a problem will never be corrected. You have to use a different way to reconcile differences rather than roughness. Responding in the same way is called confrontation. However, if you use a different way, the way of gentleness, the real conquering force is not in a man's hand but in the woman's hand.

The original purpose of the *Tao Teh Ching* was to point out the direction of human culture and also to teach people to become wise. If a leader competes with all the other men, nothing can be achieved. But if he learns to become wise and cooperative, the cooperative attitude and exchange of cooperative strength will make him a leader and he will build more strength.

In family life, it is not emotional competition for leadership that brings the results you wish. It is the correct application of gentleness and tenderness. You subtly receive leadership by doing so, but you still entitle your husband as the head of the family. This is the best strength a woman can have. If you give up this strength to imitate the man's strength, sometimes the woman is a loser. If you become provocative, you have more opportunity to receive a beating from a rough man or end in divorce. You shall never find happiness in your life by competition or confrontation. Instead, you let the roughness happen and respond with silence or say you will think about it. Then later, when things are calm, come back with a good solution to the problem, and present it in a gentle way with the spirit of appreciation for your man and his helpfulness.

When you know the problem of man, you know the problem of world, too and you can then change yourself when we narrow down the great teaching in small use. That will bring benefit to your life.

Chapter 9

Radiant Pearl

There was once a man who wandered far from his home when he was young. Traveling by boat, he eventually reached a group of islands and decided to settle on the largest of them. He became successful there in his later years, but although he had almost everything he could wish for, there were two things in life that he missed: his homeland and a spiritual path.

The island where the man lived was famous for its wealth of beautiful pearls and so was called the Island of Pearls, and, every day, good weather or poor, they dove to the bottom of the sea to gather the pearls. Only the best ones were kept; the imperfect, undeveloped ones were thrown back. The harvesting of this special product made the islanders wealthy, but they spent their leisure time enjoying only food and sex; they knew nothing higher.

There was an island girl, however, who became enlightened through her work of diving for pearls. She had realized that people, just like pearls, had both an essence and an outer shell, and that the essence was what maintained the shell. So, she concluded, if people cultivated only the shell and neglected their essence, then their lives would be wasted. She therefore worked on maintaining her essence and naturally started to practice self-cultivation. She was the only one among the islanders who changed her life to reach a higher awareness, and she developed such foresight and wisdom that she eventually became known as "Radiant Pearl."

The man who had come to the island as a traveler in his youth heard about the powers of Radiant Pearl and decided to pay her a visit. He expressed himself directly and with sincerity, "The spiritual development of these islanders does not go beyond mere idol worship. They expect to receive life's blessings, yet they are neither able to see the light of truth nor are they aware of how to cultivate themselves. But you, Radiant Pearl, have seen that light. I have come to ask you to please guide me home, spiritually as well as to my homeland on this earth."

Radiant Pearl answered the man, saying, "Although your physical home may be far away, the spiritual home of everyone is very close. If you had to choose between them, which would you want most urgently?"

The man reflected and said, "My first wish is to know my eternal home. I can search for my homeland on my own."

Radiant Pearl then replied, "Both are reached by your own searching. However, if you think you need my help, then I ask that you help me in teaching the islanders to search for their home."

The man looked blank for a moment and then said, "I know nothing about spiritual cultivation or achievement. That is why I have come to you!"

Radiant pearl smiled and said to him, "You said, just now, that these islanders knew only idol worship, and that not one among them was able to see the light or knew how to cultivate himself. If you do not know the light, then how can you recognize darkness? Am I right?"

The man thought and then said, "In my homeland, I heard a few words once about the Great Path of One Truth. They were like a seed planted in my being. It is always with me, but I do not know how to encourage its growth."

Radiant Pearl said, "I would appreciate it very much if you would share those words with me."

The man exclaimed, "Gladly! What I remember is that the Great Path of One Truth is the path of subtle integration. Its purpose is the spiritual integration of individuals and society. It is the path of All-Embracing Oneness and the path of the growth of wisdom. It is the path of virtuous fulfillment, not the projection of primitive impulses onto an image which can be materially and conceptually worshipped. The Great Path of One Truth contains hope for the spiritual progress of the whole world.

"This is all I can remember. I came to you in the hope that you could help me cultivate myself in a natural way so that I could realize the Great Path in my own life.'

Radiant Pearl said to the man, "What you have described is what I contemplate daily. I have a great desire to find one who can teach the Great Path so that I may test the correctness of my own personal cultivation."

The man's face lit up with joy. "Excellent!" He exclaimed. "It seems that we share the same deep wish. We must go together to look for this great teacher and keep looking until we find him!" After a long discussion, they agreed to start their spiritual journey together. One morning, just before dawn, they set out on their search.

After much traveling and searching, the man and Radiant Pearl heard of a young teacher of the Great Path who had been seen teaching by the ocean. This teacher was known to have traveled widely, so they hoped that he would also be able to guide the man back to his homeland. When they finally found him, they bowed respectfully, seeing his great light with their spiritual eyes. The young teacher looked from one to the other and said, "What is it you wish to know?"

The man said, "I do not know how to find my way back to the home of my ancestors and I hope that you can help me. But I also wish to find my eternal home and help others do the same. I know of your high achievement and have heard that you spread your teachings throughout the world. We want to learn the Great Path of All-Embracing Oneness and deliver the people of our island from the darkness that keeps them from its virtuous practice."

After a short pause the teacher said, "You have great wisdom, virtue and courage. The enlightenment of superstitious islanders is no easy task."

The man bowed before the teacher and said, "Thank you for your confidence in me, but please allow me to present one whose virtue and knowledge is greater than mine. This is Radiant Pearl; she is from the islands I spoke of, but she has learned from her own experience and is naturally wise. She has also been diligent in not letting her mind return to the spiritual backwardness of the islanders she lives among."

The teacher then turned and said to Radiant Pearl, "Please, come forward and speak."

Radiant Pearl said simply, in a clear voice, "Please tell me about the Great Path of One Truth."

The young teacher responded to her in an equally direct manner, saying, "The Great Path distinguishes between mankind's search for spiritual development and the invention of conceptual tools that are used for ruling people. The Great Path taches that the universe is one huge body; all the galaxies, constellations, stars and planets together are its form, with the living being of a person as a small model and portion of this body. The three spheres of human life (body, mind and spirit) parallel those of the universe itself (universal body, universal mind and universal spirit) and they function as an integral whole, both in the universal and the individual, human body. Thus, although the collective universe and the human being appear to be two, in reality they are an integral unit, inseparable from one another.

"This is clear to an achieved one, but most people, unfortunately, do not know it. Those who are blocked by their own ignorance pursue only sensual expression and enjoyment and fail to seek the completeness of life. Full development of body, mind and spirit requires a balance between intuition, intellect and emotion. I have a clear vision of this wisdom being passed on through you. This may sound far-fetched to some, but to those of integral vision it will be obvious. One equipped with the wisdom of the Great Path must surely become the Great One.

"A human life without spiritual achievement is like an empty shell left on the shore of the vast ocean or like an oyster without a pearl. Those of spiritual achievement who gather the essence from the rough shell of their own personalities and the material world succeed in cultivating pearls of radiant light that express the essence of the universe. One can uplift oneself by refining the coarseness of his or her personal energy and transforming it into everlasting spiritual essence.

"A woman's life has many obstacles, but one can swiftly overcome them to achieve the luminous pearls which can light up the world. A person of simplicity like this young girl can verify the truth as well as many men of great learning or wisdom. Women of spiritual achievement shall sit on the seat above the lotus flower and be showered with pearls which will enable them to awaken all people through the teachings of the Great Path. My friends, each of you has your own pearl which you can cultivate and offer to the world; such a life is worth living."

The man and Radiant Pearl bowed their heads and Radiant Pearl said, "Compassionate Teacher, you have revealed the Great Path to me and for that I am deeply grateful. I know now that there is no difference between it and my own true nature, yet I feel inadequate to be a teacher of this path. I do not know how to put the truth into words; it is difficult to express. I only know about pearls. Can one compare the integralness of truth to the wholeness of a beautiful pearl? I do not know the correct approach to take, and I am afraid that if I leave something out, then just like a broken pearl which has no value, the incomplete truth will also be of little worth to people."

The teacher said, "You are a person of truth, Radiant Pearl; you are one among millions, an you have my deepest respect. May I know how you came to reach such high level of spiritual achievement?"

Radiant Pearl bowed her head and said, "Great Teacher, I am not aware of the level of my achievement; I did not know there were different levels. There is no difference between one who knows the truth and one who does not, because our nature is the truth. There is a great difference, however, between one who lives by the truth and one who does not. Therefore, the knowledge of truth is valuable, and teachers are important instruments for conveying it.

"As for my own spiritual development, I was inspired by the luminous beauty of the pearls. They were the most beautiful and valuable things I had ever touched in my whole life. What I know, therefore, is not higher than a pearl. I have learned everything from them. When I was young, the way a pearl formed inside an oyster and grew into a beautiful, smooth, whole essence inspired me to strive for that same perfection. The oyster conceives a pearl just like a mother conceives a baby, according to a monthly cycle, for pearls, just like human beings, are responsive to moonlight. Some are formed over many long years and have great spiritual powers. Their natural energy, converged into a marvelous shape, gives them a unique and precious value that can never be expressed in words. There is the Pearl of Illuminating the Night which can light up a large room so brightly that a single hair in the eyebrow of someone across the room can easily be distinguished. The Pearl of Water-Yielding can be sewn into the pocket of an undergarment so that if one falls into water it will clear a path through the water for him an he may take the ocean's wealth as easily as picking ripe fruit form a tree. With the Pearl of Wind-Yielding one can light a fire in the strongest wind, and yet the flame will remain stable and constant. Then there is the Pearl of Devil-Frightening; with it one is free and safe from any evil force. The Pearl of All-Curing is used to heal the sick and dying; if one rubs it on the person's lips, recovery will be complete and whoever carries this pearl becomes immune to all disease or negative energy.

"It is the dream of every diver to find such a pearl, but I do not know anyone who has. I have been told that such pearls as these can only be obtained by people of great virtue. One of my ancestors had one, but unfortunately it was lost in later generations. If we still had it, I would have liked to have offered it to you."

The young teacher said, "Thank you for your kindness Radiant Pearl, but I think you will be happy to know that I already have one of these. It is even more powerful than the ones you have just mentioned, for it can never be lost or stolen. I can show it only to one who knows pearls. Please look at my pearl by listening:

> *This person has achieved himself*
> *   with the Path of the Mystical Pearl.*
> *He has accomplished the refinement of*
> *   the great Mystical Pearl in whose reflection*
> *   the guest and the host can be distinctly seen.*
> *Its voice is as strong as a lion's,*
> *   and what it says is not common sense.*
> *Sometimes it turns around by itself*
> *   in great joy.*

Because its power is so marvelous,
    it teaches with authority.
It can explain the path in two ways:
the direct and the direct in the indirect.
When an Achieved One obtains it,
    it displays a wondrous power.
In the hands of an undeveloped one
    it is of little use.

The pearl of the mind is like
    moonlight on water:
There is not the slightest difference between
    the thousand sparks of light
    on the water's surface
    and the moon itself, high above.
A difference can be seen, however,
    between the enlightened and the lost.
The Kind One, therefore, finds many ways
    to tell of hell and hungry ghosts.
The six tunnels of reincarnation
    offer no place for one of truth
    to set his steps.
It is not the unmercifulness of the Great Divine
    that breaks them all:
It is the King of the Shadow World
    who fears to face the truth.

Oh dear friends, think deeply;
    do not abuse this precious jewel of yours.
If one does not know the false
    and fragile structure of this shallow life,
Then how can one find the pearl again
    after the body has disintegrated?

When the young teacher had finished speaking, Radiant
Pearl and the man sat for a long time in deep meditation,
and they both heard the subtle, unsounded guidance of the
Heavenly beings:

The one who knows
how to glean the Mystical Pearl
can dissolve all troubles.
With it he can attain eternal truth
and enter the pure spiritual realm.
The unrevealed subtle truth of life
always manifests itself in daily life.
Have the ancient books
not taught you enough?

Palaces, pavilions, towers and terraces
are not the expressions of true life.
Things of external beauty and grandeur
cannot sustain your life.
Once the essence of your life is scattered,
what is the value of ornamental forms?
Once the Mystical Pearl is thrown away,
you have nothing else.

The dusty mind cannot see Heaven
in its own body.
Everywhere people wish to reach the truth
through conventional religion.
They do not know they have
their own Mystical pearl.
To find it, one must return to his own field,
Where the immortal herb grows.

Sometime later the teacher turned to the man and said, "My friend, you have spent a long time looking for your homeland; the road is beneath your feet. Everyone can find the road home, for when one reaches spiritual enlightenment, one is home."

Then, speaking to both the man and to Radiant Pearl, he said, "You have been to the small islands of the vast ocean and seen the chaos and alienation of an undeveloped way of life. You and I, my friends, can work in these islands and this ocean. I am referring to the ocean of human society and the islands of isolated individuals who have separated themselves from each other by misunderstanding their own nature. They do not realize that we all depend on one another and were meant to live in peaceful cooperation, working as an integrated whole, like the drops of water in an ocean. Only in this way can a true society be built, with the wisdom that unites human intelligence in consideration for both the individual and society. Cooperation mans co-existence, while competition brings only destruction.

"I wish to bring you both to meet the Great One of the Great Path of One Truth. Take these books of the Great One's teachings and follow their guidance, for they convey invaluable truths."

With this precious gift, the man and Radiant Pearl took their leave of the great teacher.

> *"All under Heaven come to see*
> *the one who embraces the great,*
> *unadorned truth in guiding people.*
> *Those who follow him are free from harm*
> *and enjoy peace and security.*
> *The teaching of the path of subtle*
> *universal integration is like plain but healthy*
> *food to those who travel in search of truth.*
>
> *When the path of subtle universal integration*
> *is told orally, it has no special flavor or taste.*
> *When looked at, it has no distinctive beauty.*
> *When listened to, it has no particular sound.*
> *But, when put to use, it is always competent."*

Reprinted from *The Uncharted Voyage Toward the Subtle Light*

About Taoist Master Ni, Hua Ching

Master Ni, Hua-Ching is fully acknowledged and empowered as a true Master of Tao. He is heir to the wisdom transmitted through an unbroken succession of 74 generations of Taoist Masters dating back to 216 B.C. As a young boy, he was educated within his family and then studied more than 31 years in the high mountains of China, fully achieving all aspects of Taoist science and metaphysics.

In addition, 38 generations of the Ni family have practiced natural Taoist medicine. Master Ni has continued this in America with clinics and the establishment of Yo San University of Traditional Chinese Medicine.

As a young boy, Master Ni, Hua-Ching was educated by his family in the spiritual foundation of Tao. Later, he learned Taoist arts from various achieved teachers, some of whom have a long traditional background. Master Ni worked as a traditional Chinese doctor and taught Taoist learning on the side as a service to people. He taught first in Taiwan for 27 years by offering many publications in Chinese and then in the United States and other Western countries since 1976. To date, he has published about 18 books in English, made five videotapes of Taoist movements and wrote several dozen Taoist songs sung by an American singer.

Master Ni stayed about 31 years in the mountains in different stages. He thinks the best way to live, when possible, is to be part-time in seclusion in the mountains and part-time in the city doing work of a different nature. He believes this is better for the nervous system than staying only in one type of environment.

The 50 books that Master Ni has written in Chinese include 2 books about Chinese medicine, 5 books about Taoist spiritual cultivation and 4 books about the Chinese internal school of martial arts. The above were published in Taiwan. He has also written two unpublished books on Taoist subjects.

The other unpublished 33 books were written by brush in Chinese calligraphy during the years he attained a certain degree of achievement in his personal spiritual cultivation. Master Ni said, "Those books were written when my spiritual energy was rising to my head to answer the deep questions in my mind. In spiritual self-cultivation, only by nurturing your own internal spirit can communication exist between the internal and external gods. This can be proven by your personal spiritual stature. For example, after nurturing your internal spirit, through your thoughts, you contact many subjects which you could not reach in ordinary daily life. Such spiritual inspiration comes to help when you need it. Writings done in good concentration are almost like meditation and are one fruit of your cultivation. This type of writing is how internal and external spiritual communication can be realized. For the purpose of self-instruction, writing is one important practice of the Jing Ming School or the School of Pure Light. It was beneficial to me as I grew spiritually. I began to write when I was a teenager and my spiritual self awareness had begun to grow."

In his books published in Taiwan, Master Ni did not give the details of his spiritual background. It was ancient Taoist custom that all writers, such as Lao Tzu and Chuang Tzu, avoided giving their personal description. Lao Tzu and Chuang Tzu were not even their names. However, Master Ni conforms with the modern system of biographies and copyrights to meet the needs of the new society.

Master Ni's teaching differs from what is generally called Taoism in modern times. There is no comparison or relationship between his teaching and conventional folk Taoism. Master Ni describes his independent teaching as having been trained without the narrow concept of lineage or religious mixture of folk Taoism. It is non-conventional and differs from the teaching of any other teachers.

Master Ni shares his own achievement as the teaching of rejuvenated Taoism, which has its origins in the prehistoric stages of human life. Master Ni's teaching is the Integral Way or Integral Taoism. It is based on the Three Scriptures of Taoist Mysticism: Lao Tzu's *Tao Teh Ching, The Teachings of Chuang Tzu* and *The I Ching (The Book of Changes)*. Master Ni has translated these three classics into versions which carry the accuracy of the most valuable ancient message. His other books are materials for different stages of learning Tao. He has also absorbed all the truthful and highest spiritual achievements from various schools to assist the illustration of Tao with his own achieved insight on those different levels of teachings.

The ancient Taoist writing contained in the Three Scriptures of Taoist Mysticism and all Taoist books of many schools were very difficult to understand, even for Chinese scholars. Thus, the real Taoist teaching is not known to most scholars of later generations, the Chinese people or foreign translators. It would have become lost to the world if Master Ni, with his spiritual achievement, had not rewritten it and put it into simple language. He has practically revived the ancient teaching to make it useful for all people.

It is the true, traditional spirit of the teaching of Tao, different from some leaders in later times who made it as the mixed Taoist religion. Toward society, the teaching of Tao serves as public spiritual education. Toward individuals, the teaching guides internal spiritual prctice. Therefore, the true teaching of Tao has nothing to do with any religions which use formality and damage the true, independent spirit. Although some traditional practice has some external layout, it is the symbol of spiritual practice and some postures which are for guiding or conducting energy in the body. Since its beginnings, this true tradition of Tao has been independent of social limitation. It has also never been involved with the competition of any social religion because this tradition's goal is to help the spiritual development of individuals, broad human society, all religion and culture. Its spiritual teaching is above the confusion of custom and fashionable thought which happens in the frame of time and location. The teaching of Tao serves a deeper and higher sphere of limited life.

Throughout the world, Master Ni teaches the simple, pure message of his spiritual ancestors to assist modern people understand life and awakening to Tao. Taoist Master Ni, Hua-Ching has spoken out and clearly offered more teaching than any other true Taoist master in history. With his achieved insight, over 80 years of training and teaching, and his deep spiritual commitment, Master Ni shares his own achievement as the pure rejuvenated teaching of the Integral Tao.

This list of Master Ni's books in English is ordered by date of publication for those readers who wish to follow the sequence of his Western teaching material in their learning of Tao.

1979:   *The Complete Works of Lao Tzu*
        The Taoist Inner View of the Universe
        Tao, the Subtle Universal Law
1983:   *The Book of Changes and the Unchanging Truth*
        8,000 Years of Wisdom, I
        8,000 Years of Wisdom, II
1984:   *Workbook for Spiritual Development*
1985:   *The Uncharted Voyage Towards the Subtle Light*
1986:   *Footsteps of the Mystical Child*
1987:   *The Gentle Path of Spiritual Progress*
        Spiritual Messages from a Buffalo Rider, (originally
                part of *Gentle Path of Spiritual Progress*)
1989:   *The Way of Integral Life*
        Enlightenment: Mother of Spiritual Independence
        Attaining Unlimited Life
        The Story of Two Kingdoms
1990:   *Stepping Stones for Spiritual Success*
        Guide to Inner Light
        Essence of Universal Spirituality
1991:   *Internal Growth through Tao*
        Nurture Your Spirits
        Quest of Soul
        Power of Natural Healing
        *Attune Your Body with Dao-In: Taoist Exercise for a Long and
                Happy Life*
        Eternal Light
        Harmony: The Art of Life
        The Key to Good Fortune: Refining Your Spirit
        Moonlight in the Dark Night

In addition, the forthcoming books will be compiled from his lecturing and teaching service:

Golden Message: The Tao in Your Daily Life (by Daoshing and
        Maoshing Ni, based on the works of Master Ni, Hua-Ching)
Learning Gentle Path T'ai Chi Chuan
Learning Sky Journey T'ai Chi Chuan
Learning Infinite Expansion T'ai Chi Chuan
Learning Cosmic Tour Ba Gua
The Mystical Universal Mother
Taoist Mysticism: The Uniting of God and Human Life
Life and Teachings of Two Immortals, Volume I: Kou Hong
Life and Teachings of Two Immortals, Volume II: Chen Tuan

BOOKS IN ENGLISH BY MASTER NI

Moonlight in the Dark Night - *New Publication!*
In order to attain inner clarity and freedom of the soul, you have to get your emotions under control. It seems that spiritual achievement itself is not a great obstacle, once you understand what is helpful and what is not. What is left for most people is their own emtions, which affect the way they treat themselvs and others. This will cause trouble for themselvs or for other people. This book contains Taoist wisdom on the balancing of the emotions, including balancing love relationships, so that spiritual achievement can become possible. 168 pages, softcover, Stock No. BMOON, $12.95

Harmony - The Art of Life - *New Publication!*
Harmony occurs when two different things find the point at which they can link together. The point of linkage, if healthy and helpful, brings harmony. Harmony is a spiritual matter which relates to each individual's personal sensitivity and the sensitivity of each situation of daily life. Basically, harmony comes from understanding yourself. In this book, Master Ni shares some valuable Taoist understanding and insight about the ability to bring harmony within one's own self, one's relationships and the world. 208 pages, Stock No. BHARM, softcover, $14.95

Attune Your Body With Dao-In: Taoist Exercise for a Long and Happy Life
- *New Publication!* - Dao-In is a series of typical Taoist movements which are traditionally used for physical energy conducting. These exercises were passed down from the ancient achieved Taoists and immortals. The ancients discovered that Dao-In exercises not only solved problems of stagnant energy, but also increased their health and lengthened their years. The exercises are also used as practical support for cultivation and the higher achievements of spiritual immortality. 144 pages, BDAOI Softcover with photographs, $14.95

The Key to Good Fortune: Refining Your Spirit - *New Publication!*
A translation of Straighten Your Way (Tai Shan Kan Yin Pien) and The Silent Way of Blessing (Yin Chia Wen), which are the main guidance for a mature and healthy life. This amplified version of the popular booklet called The Heavenly Way includes a new commentary section by Master Ni which discusses how spiritual improvement can become an integral part of one's life and how to realize a Heavenly life on earth. 144 pages. Stock No. BKEYT. Softcover, $12.95

Eternal Light - *New Publication!*
In this book, Master Ni presents the life and teachings of his father, Grandmaster Ni, Yo San, who was a spiritually achieved person, a Taoist healer and teacher, and a source of inspiration to Master Ni in his life. Here is an intimate look at the lifestyle of

a spiritual family. Some of the deeper teachings and understandings of spirituality passed from father to son are clearly given and elucidated. This book is recommended for those committed to living a spiritual way of life and wishing for higher achievement. 208 pages Stock No. BETER Softcover, $14.95

Quest of Soul - *New Publication!*
In Quest of Soul, Master Ni addresses many subjects relevant to understanding one's own soul, such as the religious concept of saving the soul, how to improve the quality of the personal soul, the high spiritual achievement of free soul, what happens spiritually at death and the universal soul. He guides the reader into deeper knowledge of oneself and inspires each individual to move forward to increase both one's own personal happiness and spiritual level. 152 pages. Stock No. BQUES Softcover, $11.95

Nurture Your Spirits - *New Publication!*
With truthful spiritual knowledge, you have better life attitudes that are more supportive to your existence. With truthful spiritual knowledge, nobody can cause you spiritual confusion. Where can you find such advantage? It would take a lifetime of develop-ment in a correct school, but such a school is not available. However, in this book, Master Ni breaks some spiritual prohibitions and presents the spiritual truth he has studied and proven. This truth may help you develop and nurture your own spirits which are the truthful internal foundation of your life being. Taoism is educational; its purpose is not to group people to build social strength but to help each individual build one's own spiritual strength. 176 pages. Stock No. BNURT Softcover, $12.95

Internal Growth Through Tao - *New Publication!*
Material goods can be passed from one person to another, but growth and awareness cannot be given in the same way. Spiritual development is related to one's own internal and external beingness. Through books, discussion or classes, wise people are able to use others' experiences to kindle their own inner light to help their own growth and live a life of no separation from their own spiritual nature. In this book, Master Ni teaches the more subtle, much deeper sphere of the reality of life that is above the shallow sphere of external achievement. He also shows the confusion caused by some spiritual teachings and guides you in the direction of developing spiritually by growing internally. 208 pages. Stock No. BINTE Softcover, $13.95

Power of Natural Healing - *New Publication!*
Master Ni discusses the natural capability of self-healing in this book, which is healing physical trouble untreated by medication or external measure. He offers information and practices which can assist any treatment method currently being used by someone seeking health. He goes deeper to discuss methods of Taoist cultivation which promote a healthy life, including Taoist spiritual achievement, which brings about health and longevity. This book is not only suitable for a person seeking to improve one's health condition. Those who wish to live long and happy, and to understand more

about living a natural healthy lifestyle, may be supported by the practice of Taoist energy cultivation. 230 pages. Stock No. BHEAL Softcover, $14.95

Essence of Universal Spirituality

In this volume, as an open-minded learner and achieved teacher of universal spirituality, Master Ni examines and discusses all levels and topics of religious and spiritual teaching to help you develop your own correct knowledge of the essence existing above the differences in religious practice. He reviews religious teachings with hope to benefit modern people. This book is to help readers to come to understand the ultimate truth and enjoy the achievement of all religions without becoming confused by them. 304 pages. Stock No. BESSE Softcover, $19.95

Guide to Inner Light

Modern life is controlled by city environments, cultural customs, religious teachings and politics that can all divert our attention away from our natural life being. As a result, we lose the perspective of viewing ourselves as natural completeness. This book reveals the development of ancient Taoist adepts. Drawing inspiration from their experience, modern people looking for the true source and meaning of life can find great teachings to direct and benefit them. The invaluable ancient Taoist development can teach us to reach the attainable spiritual truth and point the way to the Inner Light. Master Ni uses the ancient high accomplishments to make this book a useful resource. 192 pages. Stock No. BGUID. Softcover, $12.95

Stepping Stones for Spiritual Success

In Asia, the custom of foot binding was followed for close to a thousand years. In the West, people did not practice foot binding, but they bound their thoughts for a much longer period, some 1,500 to 1,700 years. Their mind and thinking became unnatural. Being unnatural expresses a state of confusion where people do not know what is right. Once they become natural again, they become clear and progress is great. Master Ni invites his readers to unbind their minds; in this volume, he has taken the best of the traditional teachings and put them into contemporary language to make them more relevant to our time, culture and lives. 160 pages. Stock No. BSTEP. Softcover, $12.95.

The Complete Works of Lao Tzu

Lao Tzu's Tao Teh Ching is one of the most widely translated and cherished works of literature in the world. It presents the core of Taoist philosophy. Lao Tzu's timeless wisdom provides a bridge to the subtle spiritual truth and practical guidelines for harmonious and peaceful living. Master Ni has included what is believed to be the only English translation of the Hua Hu Ching, a later work of Lao Tzu which has been lost to the general public for a thousand years. 212 pages. Stock No. BCOMP. Softcover, $12.95

Order The Complete Works of Lao Tzu and the companion Tao Teh Ching Cassette Tapes for only $23.00. Stock No. ABTAO.

The Book of Changes and the Unchanging Truth
The first edition of this book was widely appreciated by its readers, who drew great spiritual benefit from it. They found the principles of the I Ching to be clearly explained and useful to their lives, especially the helpful commentaries. The legendary classic I Ching is recognized as mankind's first written book of wisdom. Leaders and sages throughout history have consulted it as a trusted advisor which reveals the appropriate action to be taken in any of life's circumstances. This volume also includes over 200 pages of background material on Taoist principles of natural energy cycles, instruction and commentaries. New, revised second edition, 669 pages. Stock No. BBOOK. Hardcover, $35.50

The Story of Two Kingdoms
This volume is the metaphoric tale of the conflict between the Kingdoms of Light and Darkness. Through this unique story, Master Ni transmits the esoteric teachings of Taoism which have been carefully guarded secrets for over 5,000 years. This book is for those who are serious in their search and have devoted their lives to achieving high spiritual goals. 122 pages. Stock No. BSTOR. Hardcover, $14.50

The Way of Integral Life
This book can help build a bridge for those wishing to connect spiritual and intellectual development. It is most helpful for modern educated people. It includes practical and applicable suggestions for daily life, philosophical thought, esoteric insight and guidelines for those aspiring to give help and service to the world. This book helps you learn the wisdom of the ancient sages' achievement to assist the growth of your own wisdom and integrate it as your own new light and principles for balanced, reasonable living in worldly life. 320 pages. Softcover, $14.00, Stock No. BWAYS. Hardcover, $20.00, Stock No. BWAYH

Enlightenment: Mother of Spiritual Independence
The inspiring story and teachings of Master Hui Neng, the father of Zen Buddhism and Sixth Patriarch of the Buddhist tradition, highlight this volume. Hui Neng was a person of ordinary birth, intellectually unsophisticated, who achieved himself to become a spiritual leader. Master Ni includes enlivening commentaries and explanations of the principles outlined by this spiritual revolutionary. Having received the same training as all Zen Masters as one aspect of his training and spiritual achievement, Master Ni offers this teaching so that his readers may be guided in their process of spiritual development. 264 pages. Softcover, $12.50, Stock No. BENLS. Hardcover, $22.00, Stock No. BENLH

Attaining Unlimited Life
The thought-provoking teachings of Chuang Tzu are presented in this volume. He was perhaps the greatest philosopher and master of Taoism and he laid the foundation for the Taoist school of thought. Without his work, people of later generations would hardly recognize the value of Lao Tzu's teaching in practical, everyday life. He touches the organic nature of human life more deeply and directly than that of other great teachers. This volume also includes questions by students and answers by Master Ni. 467 pages. Softcover, $18.00, Stock No. BATTS; Hardcover, $25.00, Stock No. BATTH

Special Discount: Order the three classics Way of Integral Life, Enlightenment: Mother of Spiritual Independence *and* Attaining Unlimited Light *in the hardbound editions, Stock No. BHARD for $60.00.*

The Gentle Path of Spiritual Progress
This book offers a glimpse into the dialogues of a Taoist master and his students. In a relaxed, open manner, Master Ni, Hua-Ching explains to his students the fundamental practices that are the keys to experiencing enlightenment in everyday life. Many of the traditional secrets of Taoist training are revealed. His students also ask a surprising range of questions, and Master Ni's answers touch on contemporary psychology, finances, sexual advice, how to use the I Ching as well as the telling of some fascinating Taoist legends. Softcover, $12.95, Stock No. BGENT

Spiritual Messages from a Buffalo Rider, A Man of Tao
This is another important collection of Master Ni's service in his worldly trip, originally published as one half of The Gentle Path. He had the opportunity to meet people and answer their questions to help them gain the spiritual awareness that we live at the command of our animal nature. Our buffalo nature rides on us, whereas an achieved person rides the buffalo. In this book, Master Ni gives much helpful knowledge to those who are interested in improving their lives and deepening their cultivation so they too can develop beyond their mundane beings. Softcover, $12.95, Stock No. BSPIR

8,000 Years of Wisdom, Volume I and II
This two volume set contains a wealth of practical, down-to-earth advice given by Master Ni to his students over a five year period, 1979 to 1983. Drawing on his training in Traditional Chinese Medicine, Herbology, Acupuncture and other Taoist arts, Master Ni gives candid answers to students' questions on many topics ranging from dietary guidance to sex and pregnancy, meditation techniques and natural cures for common illnesses. Volume I includes dietary guidance; 236 pages; Stock No. BWIS1 Volume II includes sex and pregnancy guidance; 241 pages; Stock No. BWIS2. Softcover, Each Volume $12.50

Special discount: Order both Book I and Book II of 8,000 Years of Wisdom, Stock No. BWIS3, for $22.00.

The Uncharted Voyage Towards the Subtle Light

Spiritual life in the world today has become a confusing mixture of dying traditions and radical novelties. People who earnestly and sincerely seek something more than just a way to fit into the complexities of a modern structure that does not support true self-development often find themselves spiritually struggling. This book provides a profound understanding and insight into the underlying heart of all paths of spiritual growth, the subtle origin and the eternal truth of one universal life. 424 pages. Stock No. BUNCH. Softcover, $14.50

The Heavenly Way

A translation of the classic Tai Shan Kan Yin Pien (Straighten Your Way) and Yin Chia Wen (The Silent Way of Blessing). The treaties in this booklet are the main guidance for a mature and healthy life. The purpose of this booklet is to promote the recognition of truth, because only truth can teach the perpetual Heavenly Way by which one reconnects oneself with the divine nature. 41 pages. Stock No. BHEAV. Softcover, $2.50

Special Discount: Order the Heavenly Way in a set of 10 - great for gifts or giveaways. (One shipping item). BHIV10 $17.50.

Footsteps of the Mystical Child

This book poses and answers such questions as: What is a soul? What is wisdom? What is spiritual evolution? The answers to these and many other questions enable readers to open themselves to new realms of understanding and personal growth. There are also many true examples about people's internal and external struggles on the path of self-development and spiritual evolution. 166 pages. Stock No. BFOOT. Softcover, $9.50

Workbook for Spiritual Development

This book offers a practical, down-to-earth, hands-on approach for those who are devoted to the path of spiritual achievement. The reader will find diagrams showing fundamental hand positions to increase and channel one's spiritual energy, postures for sitting, standing and sleeping cultivation as well as postures for many Taoist invocations. The material in this workbook is drawn from the traditional teachings of Taoism and summarizes thousands of years of little known practices for spiritual development. An entire section is devoted to ancient invocations, another on natural celibacy and another on postures. In addition, Master Ni explains the basic attitudes and understandings that are the foundation for Taoist practices. 224 pages. Stock No. BWORK. Softcover, $12.95

Poster of Master Lu

Color poster of Master Lu, Tung Ping (shown on cover of workbook), for use with the workbook or in one's shrine. 16" x 22"; Stock No. PMLTP. $10.95

Order the Workbook for Spiritual Development *and the companion Poster of Master Lu for $18.95.* Stock No. BPWOR.

The Taoist Inner View of the Universe

This presentation of Taoist metaphysics provides guidance for one's own personal life transformation. Master Ni has given all the opportunity to know the vast achievement of the ancient unspoiled mind and its transpiercing vision. This book offers a glimpse of the inner world and immortal realm known to achieved Taoists and makes it understandable for students aspiring to a more complete life. 218 pages. Stock No. BTAOI. Softcover, $14.95

Tao, the Subtle Universal Law

Most people are unaware that their thoughts and behavior evoke responses from the invisible net of universal energy. The real meaning of Taoist self-discipline is to harmonize with universal law. To lead a good stable life is to be aware of the actual conjoining of the universal subtle law with every moment of our lives. This book presents the wisdom and practical methods that the ancient Chinese have successfully used for centuries to accomplish this. 165 pages. Stock No. TAOS. Softcover, $7.50

MATERIALS ON TAOIST HEALTH, ARTS AND SCIENCES

BOOKS

The Tao of Nutrition by Maoshing Ni, Ph.D., with Cathy McNease, B.S., M.H. - Working from ancient Chinese medical classics and contemporary research, Dr. Maoshing Ni and Cathy McNease have compiled an indispensable guide to natural healing. This exceptional book shows the reader how to take control of one's health through one's eating habits. This volume contains 3 major sections: the first section deals with theories of Chinese nutrition and philosophy; the second describes over 100 common foods in detail, listing their energetic properties, therapeutic actions and individual remedies. The third section lists nutritional remedies for many common ailments. This book presents both a healing system and a disease prevention system which is flexible in adapting to every individual's needs. 214 pages. Stock No. BNUTR. Softcover, $14.50

Chinese Vegetarian Delights by Lily Chuang
An extraordinary collection of recipes based on principles of traditional Chinese nutrition. Many recipes are therapeutically prepared with herbs. Diet has long been recognized as a key factor in health and longevity. For those who require restricted diets and those who choose an optimal diet, this cookbook is a rare treasure. Meat, sugar, diary products and fried foods are excluded. Produce, grains, tofu, eggs and seaweeds are imaginatively prepared. 104 pages. Stock No. BCHIV. Softcover, $7.50

Chinese Herbology Made Easy - by Maoshing Ni, Ph.D.
This text provides an overview of Oriental medical theory, in-depth descriptions of each herb category, with over 300 black and white photographs, extensive tables of individual herbs for easy reference, and an index of pharmaceutical and Pin-Yin names. The distillation of overwhelming material into essential elements enables one to focus efficiently and develop a clear understanding of Chinese herbology. This book is especially helpful for those studying for their California Acupuncture License. 202 pages. Stock No. BCHIH. Softcover, 14.50

Crane Style Chi Gong Book - By Daoshing Ni, Ph.D.
Chi Gong is a set of meditative exercises that was developed several thousand years ago by Taoists in China. It is now practiced for healing purposes, combining breathing techniques, body movements and mental imagery to guide the smooth flow of energy throughout the body. This book gives a more detailed account and study of Chi Gong than the videotape alone. It may be used with or without the videotape. Includes complete instructions and information on using Chi Gong exercise as a medical therapy. 55 pages. Stock No. BCRAN. Spiral bound $10.50

VIDEO TAPES

Physical Movement for Spiritual Learning: Dao-In Physical Art for a Long and Happy Life (VHS) - by Master Ni. Dao-In is a series of typical Taoist movements which are traditionally used for physical energy conducting. These exercises were passed down from the ancient achieved Taoists and immortals. The ancients discovered that Dao-In exercises not only solved problems of stagnant energy, but also increased their health and lengthened their years. The exercises are also used as practical support for cultivation and the higher achievements of spiritual immortality. Master Ni, Hua-Ching, heir to the tradition of the achieved masters, is the first one who releases this important Taoist practice to the modern world in this 1 hour videotape. Stock No. VDAOI VHS $59.95

T'ai Chi Chuan: An Appreciation (VHS) - by Master Ni - Different styles of T'ai Chi Ch'uan as Movement have different purposes and accomplish different results. In this long awaited videotape, Master Ni, Hua-Ching presents three styles of T'ai Chi Movement handed down to him through generations of highly developed masters. They are the "Gentle Path," "Sky Journey," and "Infinite Expansion" styles of T'ai Chi Movement. The three styles are presented uninterrupted in this unique videotape and are set to music for observation and appreciation. Stock No. VAPPR. VHS 30 minutes $49.95

Crane Style Chi Gong (VHS) - by Dr. Daoshing Ni, Ph.D.
Chi Gong is a set of meditative exercises developed several thousand years ago by ancient Taoists in China. It is now practiced for healing stubborn chronic diseases, strengthening the body to prevent disease and as a tool for further spiritual enlightenment. It combines breathing techniques, simple body movements, and mental imagery to guide the smooth flow of energy throughout the body. Chi gong is easy to learn for all ages. Correct and persistent practice will increase one's energy, relieve stress or tension, improve concentration and clarity, release emotional stress and restore general well-being. 2 hours Stock No. VCRAN. $65.95

Eight Treasures (VHS) - By Maoshing Ni, Ph.D.
These exercises help open blocks in a person's energy flow and strengthen one's vitality. It is a complete exercise combining physical stretching and toning and energy conducting movements coordinated with breathing. The Eight Treasures are an exercise unique to the Ni family. Patterned from nature, its 32 movements are an excellent foundation for Tai Chi Chuan or martial arts. 1 hour, 45 minutes. Stock No. VEIGH. $49.95

Tai Chi Chuan I & II (VHS) - By Maoshing Ni, Ph.D.
This exercise integrates the flow of physical movement with that of integral energy in the Taoist style of "Harmony," similar to the long form of Yang-style Tai Chi Chuan. Tai Chi has been practiced for thousands of years to help both physical longevity and spiritual cultivation. 1 hour each. Each Video Tape $49.95. Order both for $90.00. Stock Nos: Part I, VTAI1; Part II, VTAI2; Set of two, VTAI3.

AUDIO CASSETTES

Invocations: Health and Longevity and Healing a Broken Heart - By Maoshing Ni, Ph.D. *Updated with additional material!* This audio cassette guides the listener through a series of ancient invocations to channel and conduct one's own healing energy and vital force. "Thinking is louder than thunder." The mystical power by which all miracles are brought about is your sincere practice of this principle. 30 minutes. Stock No. AINVO. $8.95

Chi Gong for Stress Release - By Maoshing Ni, Ph.D.
This audio cassette guides you through simple, ancient breathing exercises that enable you to release day-to-day stress and tension that are such a common cause of illness today. 30 minutes. Stock No. ACHIS. $8.95

Chi Gong for Pain Management - By Maoshing Ni, Ph.D.
Using easy visualization and deep-breathing techniques that have been developed over thousands of years, this audio cassette offers methods for overcoming pain by invigorating your energy flow and unblocking obstructions that cause pain. 30 minutes. Stock No. ACHIP. $8.95

Tao Teh Ching Cassette Tapes
This classic work of Lao Tzu has been recorded in this two-cassette set that is a companion to the book translated by Master Ni. Professionally recorded and read by Robert Rudelson. 120 minutes. Stock No. ATAOT. $15.95

Order Master Ni's book, The Complete Works of Lao Tzu, and Tao Teh Ching Cassette Tapes for only $25.00. Stock No. ABTAO.

How To Order

Name:

Address:

City: State: Zip:

Phone - Daytime: Evening:

(We may telephone you if we have questions about your order.)

Qty.	Stock No.	Title/Description	Price Each	Total Price

Total amount for items ordered_____

Sales tax (CA residents only, 8-1/4%)_____

Shipping Charge (See below)_____

Total Amount Enclosed_____

Visa _____ Mastercard _____ Expiration Date _____

Card number:_____

Signature:_____

Shipping: In the US, we use UPS when possible. Please give full street address or nearest crossroads. All packages are insured at no extra charge. If shipping to more than one address, use separate shipping charges. Remember: 1 - 10 copies of Heavenly Way, Tao Teh Ching audio tapes and each book and tape are single items. Posters (up to 5 per tube) are a separate item. Please allow 2 - 4 weeks for US delivery and 6 - 10 weeks for foreign surface mail.

By Mail: Complete this form with payment (US funds only, No Foreign Postal Money Orders, please) and mail to: Union of Tao and Man, 117 Stonehaven Way, Los Angeles, CA 90049

Phone Orders: (213) 472-9970 - You may leave credit card orders anytime on our answering machine. Please speak clearly and remember to leave your full name and daytime phone number. We will call only if we have a question with your order, there is a delay or you specifically ask for phone confirmation.

Inquiries: If you have questions concerning your order, please refer to the date and invoice number on the top center of your invoice to help us locate your order swiftly.

Shipping Charges -
  Domestic Surface: First item $3.25, each additional, add $.50.
  Canada Surface: First item $3.25, each additional, add $1.00.
  Canada Air: First item $4.00, each additional, add $2.00
  Foreign Surface: First Item $3.50, each additional, add $2.00.
  Foreign Air: First item $12.00, each additional, add $7.00.

For the Trade: Wholesale orders may be placed direct to publisher, or with NewLeaf, BookPeople, The Distributors, Inland Books, GreatWay in US or DeepBooks in Europe.

Thank you for your order

Spiritual Study Through the College of Tao

The College of Tao and the Union of Tao and Man were established formally in California in the 1970's. This tradition is a very old spiritual culture of mankind, holding long experience of human spiritual growth. Its central goal is to offer healthy spiritual education to all people of our society. This time tested tradition values the spiritual development of each individual self and passes down its guidance and experience.

Master Ni carries his tradition from its country of origin to the west. He chooses to avoid making the mistake of old-style religions that have rigid establishments which resulted in fossilizing the delicacy of spiritual reality. Rather, he prefers to guide the teachings of his tradition as a school of no boundary rather than a religion with rigidity. Thus, the branches or centers of this Taoist school offer different programs of similar purpose. Each center extends its independent service, but all are unified in adopting Master Ni's work as the foundation of teaching to fulfill the mission of providing spiritual education to all people.

The centers offer their classes, teaching, guidance and practices on building the groundwork for cultivating a spiritually centered and well-balanced life. As a person obtains the correct knowledge with which to properly guide himself or herself, he or she can then become more skillful in handling the experiences of daily life. The assimilation of good guidance in one's practical life brings about different stages of spiritual development.

Any interested individual is welcome to join and learn to grow for oneself. You might like to join the center near where you live, or you yourself may be interested in organizing a center or study group based on the model of existing centers. In that way, we all work together for the spiritual benefit of all people. We do not require any religious type of commitment.

The learning is life. The development is yours. The connection of study may be helpful, useful and serviceable, directly to you.

- -

Mail to: Union of Tao and Man, 117 Stonehaven Way, Los Angeles, CA 90049

_____ I wish to be put on the mailing list of the Union of Tao and Man to be notified of classes, educational activities and new publications.

Name:_____

Address:_____

City:_____State:_____Zip:_____

Herbs Used by Ancient Taoist Masters

The pursuit of everlasting youth or immortality throughout human history is an innate human desire. Long ago, Chinese esoteric Taoists went to the high mountains to contemplated nature, strengthen their bodies, empower their minds and develop their spirit. From their studies and cultivation, they gave China alchemy and chemistry, herbology and acupuncture, the I Ching, astrology, martial arts and T'ai Chi Chuan, Chi Gong and many other useful kinds of knowledge.

Most important, they handed down in secrecy methods for attaining longevity and spiritual immortality. There were different levels of approach; one was to use a collection of food herb formulas that were only available to highly achieved Taoist masters. They used these food herbs to increase energy and heighten vitality. This treasured collection of herbal formulas remained within the Ni family for centuries.

Now, through Traditions of Tao, the Ni family makes these foods available for you to use to assist the foundation of your own positive development. It is only with a strong foundation that expected results are produced from diligent cultivation.

As a further benefit, in concert with the Taoist principle of self-sufficiency, Traditions of Tao offers the food herbs along with the Union of Tao and Man's publications in a distribution opportunity for anyone serious about financial independence.

Send to: *Traditions of Tao*
            117 Stonehaven Way
            Los Angeles, CA 90049

☐ *Please send me a Traditions of Tao brochure.*

☐ *Please send me information on becoming an independent distributor of Traditions of Tao herbal products and publications.*

Name _____

Address _____

City _____*State* _____*Zip* _____

Phone (day) _____*(night)* _____

Yo San University of Traditional Chinese Medicine
"Not just a medical career, but a life-time commitment to raising one's spiritual standard."

Thank you for your support and interest in our publications and services. It is by your patronage that we continue to offer you the practical knowledge and wisdom from this venerable Taoist tradition.

Because of your sustained interest in Taoism, we formed Yo San University of Traditional Chinese Medicine, a non-profit educational institute in January 1989 under the direction of founder Master Ni, Hua-Ching. Yo San University is the continuation of 38 generations of Ni family practitioners who handed down knowledge and wisdom from fathers to sons. Its purpose is to train and graduate practitioners of the highest caliber in Traditional Chinese Medicine, which includes acupuncture, herbology and spiritual development.

We view Traditional Chinese Medicine as the application of spiritual development. Its foundation is the spiritual capability to know life, to know a person's problem and how to cure it. We teach students how to care for themselves and others, and emphasize the integration of traditional knowledge and modern science. We offer a complete Master's degree program approved by the California State Department of Education that provides an excellent education in Traditional Chinese Medicine and meets all requirements for state licensure.

We invite you to inquire into our school about a creative and rewarding career as a holistic physician. Classes are also open to persons interested only in self-enrichment. For more information, please fill out the form below and send it to:

Yo San University,
117 Stonehaven Way
Los Angeles, CA 90049

☐ Please send me information on the Masters degree program in Traditional Chinese Medicine.

☐ Please send me information on health workshops and seminars.

☐ Please send me information on continuing education for acupuncturists and health professionals.

Name _____

Address_____

City_____State_____Zip_____

Phone(day)_____(night)_____

Index of Some Topics